DATE DUE

BEATING THE GLOBAL CONSOLIDATION ENDGAME

BEATING THE GLOBAL CONSOLIDATION ENDGAME

Nine Strategies for Winning in Niches

Fritz Kroeger
Andrej Vizjak
Michael Moriarty

New York   Chicago   San Francisco   Lisbon
London   Madrid   Mexico City   Milan   New Delhi
San Juan   Seoul   Singapore   Sydney Toronto

The *McGraw-Hill* Companies

1 2 3 4 5 6 7 8 9 0 DOC/DOC 0 9 8

ISBN: 978-0-07-159076-1
MHID: 0-07-159076-5

This publication is designed to provide accurate and authoritative information in regard to the subject matter covered. It is sold with the understanding that the publisher is not engaged in rendering legal, accounting, or other professional service. If legal advice or other expert assistance is required, the services of a competent professional person should be sought.
> —*From a declaration of principles jointly adopted by a committee of the American Bar Association and a committee of publishers.*

McGraw-Hill books are available at special quantity discounts to use as premiums and sales promotions, or for use in corporate training programs. To contact a representative please visit the Contact Us pages at www.mhprofessional.com.

To my three ladies:
Almuth, Carolin, and Isabel

■ ■ ■

To my family:
Denise, Lana, and Alan

■ ■ ■

For my wife, Joan,
and my children, Nicole and Elana

|Contents

|Acknowledgments

In the past seven years of working on the Merger Endgame Theory, the problem of niche strategies has always plagued us and our clients and stood out as an important but unanswered question. Andrej Vizjak, in the course of his responsibility for A.T. Kearney Eastern Europe, is confronted almost daily with niche companies that are grappling with global consolidation. Why do some small players survive the global Endgame consolidation, while most fall victim to it?

The answers, which are laid out in this book, are the result of two years of practical as well as empirical investigation. In addition to our work with niche fighters and global consolidators throughout Europe, Asia, and the Americas, many of our colleagues shared their insights and hands-on experience working with niche companies around the world. As a result, this book incorporates the insights of Svein Olaf Engenes, Karl Deutsch, Dolf Balkema, Gillis Jonk, Laurent Dumarest, Thomas Kratzert, Dietrich Neumann, Nikolaus Schumacher, Kirsten Bremke, Constanze Freienstein, and Martin Handschuh. Professor Max Ringlstetter, of the Catholic University of Eichstätt-Ingolstadt, contributed substantially, sharing both his theories and his hands-on consulting experience.

The empirical work was led by Johannes Fues and Thorston Kuhn, who also provided valuable editorial contributions. Dirk Pfannenschmidt developed new ways of analysis and always provided new hypotheses that enriched the results.

Cornelia Colsman, Roxanne Ryan, and Brett Hanley made sure that the case studies were up to date. Anja Mainzer, Patricia Sibo, and Jean Iverson handled the overall revisions with great patience and professionalism and, of course, we are grateful to Mary Glenn at McGraw-Hill for her enthusiastic support and close cooperation.

For all that is good and true in this book, we credit these, our hard-working colleagues. For all omissions or errors, we acknowledge responsibility.

BEATING
THE GLOBAL
CONSOLIDATION
ENDGAME

Introduction | The Truth about Niches

If you read through the various dictionary definitions for "niche," you get a lot of points of view without much clarity: "Niche: The area of a target market where a company or product is particularly strong." "Niche: Not mass-marketed." "A niche market is a focused, targetable portion (subset) of a market sector." But what is a niche in practice? What degrees of freedom does it provide a company, and what conclusions can be drawn about the strategic relevance of niches? Let's start with two examples: Cattles and Consors.

Cattles plc was established in the United Kingdom in 1958 as a consumer credit bank for clients with "insufficient credit ratings"—essentially, people who could not obtain credit from ordinary banks. The special feature of Cattles' offer was that debts would be collected not by mail but by personal visits to debtors' homes every week. The entire value chain, the entire culture, and everyone who worked for Cattles were focused on serving the "non-prime debtor." Because there are so many consumers in this target market, Cattles has been able to achieve high levels of growth and profitability. The bank is a market leader in this segment in the United Kingdom. Even the subprime loan debacle of late 2007 didn't take the air out of this FTSE 250 heavy hitter. In the highly competitive U.K. banking industry, Cattles is a very successful niche fighter.

Contrast this experience with that of Consors Bank. Consors was established in 1996 with a focus on Internet banking and was the first bank to concentrate exclusively on the Internet as its primary channel. Consors made its way to the stock market in 2001, and for a while it achieved clear market leadership in its segment. However, the company was ultimately forced out of the market by the resilient traditional banks, which also entered the Internet sales channel as second or third movers, but with considerably more scale and leverage. Consors was able to add something to the classic value chain of other banks, but it had nothing that the traditional players couldn't offer better and cheaper. The washed-up body of Consors Bank was taken over by BNP Paribas and integrated into that bank's well-developed commercial structure.

Why was one bank able to survive, while the other failed? What are the differences between the two business models?

The Merger Endgame Theory, developed by A.T. Kearney, analyzes the concentration and consolidation of industry sectors over time. The initial analysis found that niche companies are drawn into industry consolidation in the Focus Phase, at the latest. However, economic research attributes tremendous significance to niche markets and niche strategies, and considers companies pursuing niche strategies to be a very diverse group.

Nonetheless, with the increasing importance of industry consolidation—and the Merger Endgame—the question is how companies with niche strategies can survive this seemingly inexorable and pretty depressing process. Therefore, we sought a more nuanced view of niches that could provide business leaders and strategists with better information.

The Value Building Growth database, which contains data on 32,000 public and about 630,000 private companies, offers a rich framework for testing hypotheses concerning the capacity for niches to survive global consolidation and identifies which models are more or less successful. The results of the analyses can be summarized in the following five theses:

1. The worldwide industrial consolidation (Endgame) continues and threatens all companies that are not among the three global industry leaders, including all niche players.
2. Approximately 80 percent of all companies are niche players, and the overwhelming majority of them will fall victim to consolidation.
3. There are nine Endgame niche strategies that make it possible for a company to survive the global Endgame. They will be known in what follows as "stable Endgame niches."
4. Each of these stable Endgame niches is a powerful strategy for success, but each is most powerful at particular points in the consolidation process.
5. Figuring out which Endgame niches will be the most successful requires intimate knowledge of how the relevant industry sector's Endgame is going to play out.

In addition to the massive, empirical Merger Endgame Theory studies just described, A.T. Kearney has also performed studies focused on small and medium-sized businesses in Europe, and on the industrial structures of Eastern Europe. With the developments of the past few decades, these markets could be considered laboratories for Merger Endgame Theory and stable niche strategies. The results of these studies—which we discuss in detail later—emphasize the importance of niche fighters in the overall health of national economies and sector profitability. These studies also demonstrate the inherent instability that lies beneath these players' strategies if they do not take the global consolidation of their industry sectors into account.

What circumstances allow—or require—the development of niche players? Which conditions can provide them with stable success or doom them to certain failure? The classic discussions of strategy have so far not provided much help with these questions. The increasing concern about mindless scale, global consolidation, and sustainable environmental strategies, along with an appreciation for the competitive power of tailored, nuanced, sensitive, and unique strategies, are the primary reasons for considering the subject of niche growth strategy in such detail. We won't burden you with the macro- and microeconomic tectonic shifts that are allowing global consolidation to plow through every industry sector—30 or 40 years of increasingly fewer restrictions on global transfers of capital, currencies, goods, information, and labor. Our empirical study shows that whatever the cause, the result is clear: global consolidation will indeed end up with three or four global consolidators taking 60 to 70 percent of the global market share in each industry sector. This book is about what happens to the remaining 30 to 40 percent market share (still a pretty big market) and who wins, who loses, and who can pursue a stable niche strategy profitably, without a global consolidator breathing its moist breath down their necks every day.

Let's start the investigation with a little more depth on these five theses.

THESIS 1

The worldwide industrial consolidation (Endgame) continues and threatens all companies that are not among the three global industry leaders, including all niche players.

If we take the 32,000 publicly traded companies in the world, their place on the Merger Endgame Theory curve shows dramatic results: while there is a huge number of new entrants in the Opening Phase, there is an equally powerful "death spiral" as industry consolidation takes its proven course.

In the Opening Phase, as an industry sector is created and developed, there are lots of new entrants. This is driven by new technologies, new regulations, new ideas, or new consumer needs—or just crazy entrepreneurs who think, "Everyone else is doing it, so why can't we?" Whatever the catalyst, the number of players in a sector rises to about 8,900 (in this example of 32,000) in the transition from the Opening Phase to the Scale Phase, then collapses profoundly in each later phase. There is a big drop-off at the start of the Scale Phase, followed by a calamitous reduction during the Focus Phase, leaving a shockingly reduced number of companies in each sector in the Balance Phase (see Figure I-1).

Each industry sector behaves differently but ultimately follows the same course. Let's take a brief look at different sectors to demonstrate and reinforce the effect of global consolidation:

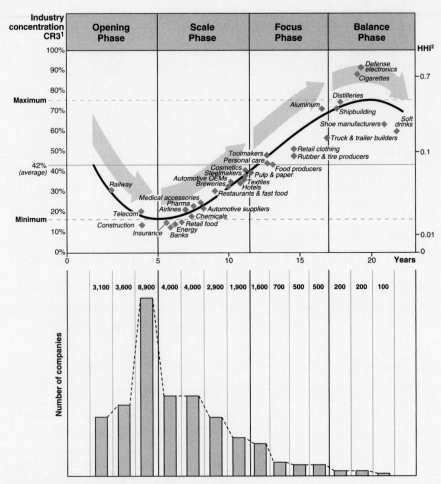

Figure I-1. Number of publicly traded companies in each Merger Endgame Theory phase

■ In the airlines sector, the small national carriers have been integrated into the large multinational airlines, and the large multinationals have created global alliances to get around regulatory barriers.

- The banking sector has experienced massive and rapid consolidation, plowing the smaller national banks into the global consolidators.
- In the brewery industry, after the EU's regulations, the consolidators began to invade even Germany's long-sequestered beer markets.
- The pharmaceutical industry has been completely reshaped. The Anglo-American and Swiss companies are now clearly the global leaders, driving previous market leaders to a lower status.
- The insurance industry has experienced a rapid and striking reorganization. In some countries this has completely changed the landscape for national and regional players.

What about the niche fighters in these sectors? With few exceptions, they have either been consolidated with the larger suppliers or disappeared completely from the market because of their inability to withstand competitive pressure. The United States' "silver bullet" brewer, Coors—for decades a countercultural icon—is now part of one of the world's largest beer groups. Air France, perhaps the most national of national airlines, has a successful partnership with KLM Royal Dutch Airlines and Delta. And where is McNeil nowadays? Rocking in the cradle of Johnson & Johnson.

THESIS 2

Approximately 80 percent of all companies are niche players, and the overwhelming majority of them will fall victim to consolidation.

What does Figure I-2 tell us about the total number of companies that will be affected by consolidation? The 32,000 public com-

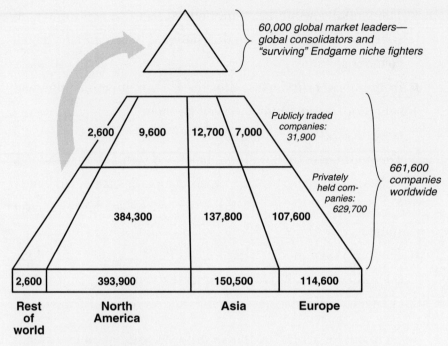

60,000 global market leaders—
global consolidators and
"surviving" Endgame niche fighters

Publicly traded
companies:
31,900

2,600   9,600   12,700   7,000

661,600
companies
worldwide

Privately
held com-
panies:
629,700

384,300   137,800   107,600

2,600   393,900   150,500   114,600

Rest   North   Asia   Europe
of   America
world

Sources: Value Building Growth database; OneSource; Amadeus; International Institute for Management Development;
World Federation of Exchanges; Jade; Orbis; A.T. Kearney analysis

Figure I-2. The Merger Endgame will lead to consolidation of
60,000 global market leaders

panies described dominate all the industry sectors and also represent—depending on the integration of the value-creation structures—about 60 to 70 percent of the GDP of any relevant national
market. If, however, we also include privately held companies, there
are an additional 630,000 companies worldwide, with the majority
of them being in North America. Obviously, data on private companies are less transparent in varying degrees and accordingly more
or less significant.

There are approximately 3,000 different industry sectors, and
three or four world market leaders in each industry sector will

emerge as global consolidators in the industrial life cycle posited
by the Merger Endgame Theory, with perhaps 10 or 12 "surviving"
niche fighters on their periphery. This means that there are currently more than 600,000 niche players that are directly threatened
by global consolidation in the coming decades.

Almost all Eastern European companies are vulnerable to this
threat, as almost none of them have the critical mass to emerge from
the Endgame as a market leader or global consolidator. This even
applies to the overwhelming majority of the Russian raw materials
companies. In addition, most small and medium-sized European,
American, and Asian enterprises will be affected.

The "hidden champions" touted by Hermann Simon, usually
medium-sized businesses that are credited with achieving lasting
success in a niche, turn out on closer inspection to be market leaders, albeit in small, stable markets. This represents relative market
shares of 2 to 4 (meaning that they are two to four times as large as
the next largest competitor) in markets with a volume of $1 billion
to $5 billion. Interestingly, some of these hidden champions have
come under the gun in the 10 years since their champion status
was announced.

There is a similar phenomenon with medium-sized businesses
in the United States and Europe, and the big start-ups in China and
India. These start-ups would be best advised to avoid direct con-
frontation with the scale leaders and to respond with a sensible
niche strategy. The Chinese government's aggregation of several
smaller retailers into the Bailian Group is a good example of this.
The government's proactive strategy will level the playing field with
multinational retail global consolidators Wal-Mart, Carrefour, and
Metro. Similarly, in India, Reliance and Aditya Birla are making

huge investments in modern retail infrastructure in anticipation of regulatory changes that are expected to open up the Indian market to wider competition.

The Merger Endgame Theory and its results from 15 years of study have shown that the number of successful small companies in the industrial consolidation curve, which is divided into 16 subsidiary stages, declines on a nearly linear basis as niche players that are unsuccessful in the long term depart from the market.

THESIS 3

The worldwide study found nine stable Endgame niche strategies that make it possible for a company to survive the global Endgame. They will be known in what follows as "stable Endgame niches."

Truly successful niche fighters are those that, for a maximum period of time, remain in the Q1 segment of the Value Building Growth matrix (see Chapter 7 for a brief description) and compete successfully with the global market leaders. These niche fighters represent 600 of the 660,000 public and private companies worldwide and form the sample for studying the success models for niche strategies, which serves as the foundation of this book.

While each of these companies has its own story, their collective experience allows us to identify nine successful niche strategies that will be referred to as stable Endgame niches. These stable niche strategies will help to ensure a company's survival and its success against the global consolidators, instead of falling into a heap of undifferentiated niche players whose chances of survival are small or at least uncertain. The companies adopting these strategies do not passively accept their fate as "niche victims," but instead assert themselves as "niche fighters" and actively take their fate in their own hands, as strongly as the market leaders strive for the consolidation of their industry sectors.

The following are summaries of the nine Endgame niches that will drive the discussion for the rest of this book.

1. Regional Niches

Some niche fighters concentrate on a clearly defined regional market. More importantly, they have a clear understanding of their target customer segments and those customers' buying habits. They solidify their market position with unique branding and customized products and services (Panafon, Jever Pilsener).

2. Target-Group Niches

These niche fighters do business globally but serve specific customers with similar needs. They focus on providing extensive and personalized service that fulfills their dedicated customers' needs. They respond to global market demand in their respective product or service areas (Sal. Oppenheim, Four Seasons Hotels).

3. Product Niches

These niche fighters also cut across international borders, but they leverage their unique product know-how and R&D capabilities to galvanize their stable Endgame niche position (Semperit).

4. Branding/Lifestyle Niches

This Endgame niche combines the power of the target-group and product niches to create communities of dedicated customers who value not only the product or service but also the company's intellectual property and the promise of value-added that the brand represents. This is a particularly powerful niche (Porsche, Montblanc, Zara).

5. Speed/Lightning-Consolidation Niches

There are a surprising number of companies that, starting from a relatively small market share, have understood that they need to concentrate on the most rapidly growing market segments. Or, through rapid consolidation over several phases of the Merger Endgame curve, these companies cut out the current market leaders, in some cases becoming global consolidators themselves. This lightning consolidation usually takes place over a relatively limited product range. Through rapid, successful consolidation, these niche fighters sometimes achieve extraordinary scale effects (ArcelorMittal, Eurokai).

6. Innovation Niches

These companies continuously and permanently change the parameters of their own industry by changing products, clients, client groups, and how regions are perceived. The emphasis here is on product innovation that gives the company a special position in the overall market. This strategy provides a strong defense for a niche company (Logitech, Zara, Apple).

7. Cooperation Niches

These interesting niche fighters create associations of smaller companies to enjoy joint economies of scale; this strategy helps companies not only survive but succeed against the global consolidators (KPMG, Ace Hardware).

8. Market-Splitting Niches

These niche fighters look at the value chain of their target industry sectors and take advantage of weaknesses in that chain as a way to enter the market, whether for components, skills, or services previously offered by current sector leaders. An example of this is the splitting of IBM's integrated IT customer offer into new and distinct markets for IT services (EDS), desktop computers (Compaq, Dell, and now Lenovo), software (SAP, Microsoft), and semiconductor chips (Intel, AMD, SIA Engineering), not to mention a lengthy roster of IT consultancies (Accenture, et al.).

9. Counter Niches

These niches are deliberately designed to supplement, complement, or compete with the market leaders. These niche fighters exploit the weaknesses or strengths of the sector leaders, forcing those leaders either to alter their strategies or risk allowing the niche fighter to "swim in the slipstream." The weaknesses (and strengths) of the market leaders are usually a result of their inflexibility, their lack of innovativeness or focus on standardization, or their inability to maintain scale advantages because of global regulatory standards. This means that specific, complementary markets are open for exploitation by counter niche fighters (Vorwerk, Tuesday Morning, United Drugs, NetJets).

Each Endgame niche provides a haven from the global consolidators at different points along the Merger Endgame curve. Some niche fighters capture incremental market share in the early Focus and Scale Phases of the Merger Endgame curve, while some niche fighters secure their chances for survival and success in the later Balance Phase of the curve (see Figure I-3).

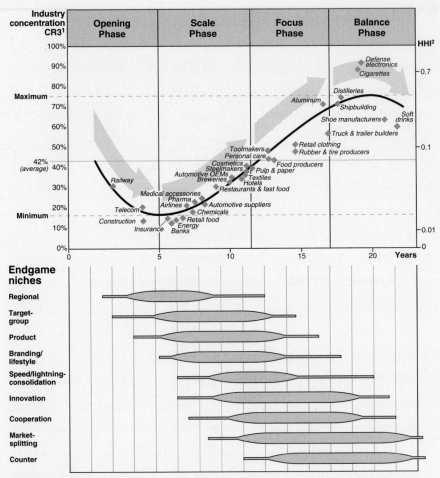

¹ CR3 = market share of the three largest companies of the total market based on the Value Building Growth database (660,000 companies).
² HHI = Hirschman-Herfindahl Index, which corresponds to the sum of the squared market shares of all companies and is greater than 90%; the axis is logarithmically plotted.
Sources: Value Building Growth database; A.T. Kearney analysis

Figure I-3. Time window of the Endgame niches by Endgame phase

Thesis 4

Each of these stable Endgame niches is a powerful strategy for success, but each is most powerful at particular points in the consolidation process.

In the Opening Phase, in which industry sectors are created and developed, all companies grow with very little focus, so niche differences are not yet very relevant and are therefore merely perceptible. Every company is on the same playing field and has an equal chance of dominating the industry sector. At this point, companies' positioning in terms of target groups, products, and regions is completely opportunistic and above all relates to the objective of growing as rapidly as possible and acquiring market volume.

This all changes in the Scale Phase, in which the industry sector begins to consolidate. In this phase, industry sectors usually strengthen their regional focus, and weak regional players are gobbled up—often without regard for the quality of the product or service offered. These acquisition decisions are usually driven by simple economics, such as the cost of capital or access to certain markets. Regional market leaders attempt to protect their positions by developing a clear understanding of their customers' taste preferences as a competitive advantage. These strategies are currently being implemented by energy suppliers, restaurant chains, and companies in the banking and insurance sectors.

Somewhat later in the Scale Phase, niche fighters have the opportunity to create a target-group niche, in which the niche fighter will concentrate on specific target groups and address them in other regions. Niche fighters then aim to grow their market shares in these segments. This Endgame niche strategy is being implemented in sectors currently going through the Focus Phase, such as retail clothing, hotel chains, and cross-regional banks.

Another strategy that niche fighters use to defend themselves against the competition is to develop special product segments, or product niche strategies, which require a specialized production or delivery process, or some other unique and differentiated approach to the value chain. This creates incremental asset value for the target customer, but it also makes these niche fighters less attractive candidates for simple scale increases—their continued survival may come into question when the industry sector moves beyond "consolidation for simple scale," but for now their position is stable and secure. Product niche fighters can be found in the pharmaceutical industry, foodstuffs producers, car suppliers, and toolmakers. This strategy helps stabilize their positions and fend off the big players.

The branding/lifestyle niche attempts to combine a target-group niche with a product niche to create a market (a "lifestyle community") of its own kind. The branding/lifestyle niche is a more powerful target-group niche because it sharpens the target-group focus in an ideological and emotional manner. This group includes trendy textile chains, cosmetics, personal-care suppliers, car and motorcycle producers, and others that are able to establish communities that can associate the consumption of a product with a specific lifestyle. Branding/lifestyle niches do not guarantee long-term protection, however, as L'Oréal's acquisition of The Body Shop demonstrates.

All of these Endgame niches—regional, target-group, product, and branding/lifestyle—have a specific window of time on the Endgame curve in which they are most effective. Regional niches lose their effectiveness around the middle of the Scale Phase, while target-group, product, and branding/lifestyle niches are effective into the Focus Phase.

Speed/lightning-consolidation niche opportunities are created as the Scale Phase begins to reach the point in which a player that is not currently a sector consolidator exploits non-sector-specific capabilities (weighted average cost of capital, regulatory changes, personal audacity). In this way, a company can rapidly consolidate the remaining sector players, at times even overtaking the current sector leaders.

To our great surprise, in our analysis we found a large number of such lightning-consolidation models in the pharmaceutical industry, the restaurant and fast-food industry, medical accessories, and among steelmakers. The aggressive Scale Phase gives the niche fighter that exploits it a running start. The power of this niche can last long into the Focus Phase.

Another Endgame niche that becomes relevant as the Scale Phase evolves is the innovation niche. Fighters that pursue an innovation niche want to survive consolidation and are also anticipating the goal of the Focus Phase, which is to optimize product offerings and improve the margin performance of the sector players. Innovation niche fighters survive and succeed by innovating with the client in mind. Product innovation may force the current market leader either to react with its own innovation or leave this "new" market sector to the niche fighter. Of course, market leaders do the latter at the risk of losing market share in the existing sector to the niche fighter. The innovation niche is one of the most frequently exploited Endgame niches. The power of this niche lasts far beyond the end of the Focus Phase.

The cooperation niche is also effective when it is employed later in the Scale Phase. This Endgame niche is also a reactive strategy, as smaller niche fighters attempt to offset the scale advantages of the sector leaders with cooperation at key points in the value chain. We have identified these niches in the pharmaceutical, automobile, and automobile supplier industries.

A variation of the cooperation niche is the market-splitting niche. Niche fighters employ this strategy by identifying elements of the sector's value chain that can be segmented and which offer the unique opportunity to create new industry sectors. This is successful in those industries that require a high level of expertise and that are already in an Endgame phase in which the market leaders are no longer as innovative or as flexible as they were in earlier phases. Successful market-splitting niche fighters create new industry sectors, restarting the Merger Endgame life cycle as the new sector creates incentives for new entrants (Opening Phase), leading to a new sequence of scale building, focus, and balance.

The final niche is the counter niche, which usually starts in the Focus Phase of the Merger Endgame life cycle. In this phase, niche fighters take advantage of the market leader's ability to sustain a defendable position, even into the Balance Phase. Counter niches can be found in the food industry, in shipbuilding, and in the aluminum industry. They can also be successful without a special industry focus.

THESIS 5

Figuring out which Endgame niches will be the most successful requires intimate knowledge of how the relevant industry sector's Endgame is going to play out.

It can easily be determined when a niche will achieve its maximum potential for success, and also when it should be sold or disposed of. Niche fighters are born when the Merger Endgame creates an opening for new businesses or a platform to capture incremental sector margins. The challenge for the niche fighter is to monitor and manage its transformation or liquidation value as closely as the global consolidators are monitoring and managing their leading role in sector consolidation.

The first step in determining whether a niche strategy can create value is to assess the industry sector's Endgame position, along with the phase that the sector is currently passing through. For example, the Scale Phase is usually too early to develop a market-splitting niche strategy, as such a strategy could be effectively rebuffed or subsumed by the market leader. Regional strategies hardly make any sense in the Focus Phase, as global economies are already integrated into the industry sector. The Endgame phase determines the outcomes for Endgame niche strategies.

By analyzing an industry sector's structure and the Value Building Growth structure, it is possible to identify the right market, product segments, and approaches for attacking that sector. All industry sectors have similarities, but each one is also unique. An intimate understanding of a sector is based on economics, culture, and history and will help determine who the future market leader will be, what its strengths and weaknesses are, and what slipstreams and neglected corners it is leaving open to exploitation.

Why did Consors fail as a niche fighter, and why is Cattles successful?

Consors, which thought the Internet would protect it from future consolidation in the banking industry, tried to distinguish itself exclusively through a sales channel niche—not an Endgame niche. All the other essential elements of Consors' value chain were those of an ordinary bank. After Consors' impressive initial successes as a first mover, the scale players entered this channel and drove Consors out with their superior scale effects. Now the essential elements of Consors' value chain are part of BNP Paribas.

Cattles attacked the established U.K. banks' strength: their orientation toward clients with good credit. In a powerful counter niche exploitation, Cattles chose to serve the subprime credit segment, which the other banks would not accept. If Cattles can maintain its economic model, and—more importantly—if the sector leaders don't decide that this target segment is one that they want to strategically pursue, Cattles can anticipate a stable Endgame niche position as a counter niche fighter today and in the future consolidation of the industry sector.

Chapter One | Is There Really Such a Thing as a "Niche Strategy"?

For companies with niche strategies, claim and reality could not be further apart. These companies cannot always predict the whole story, but they believe that they have a few successful chapters written. The ambition of niche strategists is to find small unserved or underserved markets in a sector in which they can possibly survive and succeed comfortably. "We are pursuing a long-term niche strategy" is a phrase that is frequently heard from small and medium-sized companies that can usually withstand the aggressive pressure of the scale-empowered global consolidators for only a short time. We have to ask the executives of these companies whether their niche strategy has legs in light of a fairly routine parade of failures. Not all strategies are created equal, and, as we have seen, most niche strategies are untenable in the longer term, or even the short term.

The fact is that with the alibi of a niche strategy, a lot of management's failures and mistakes are concealed. Low growth, inappropriate market segments, inadequate penetration, disadvantages of scale, and high costs are all explained away with statements such as, "We're a niche player" to divert attention from their own strategic disorientation. The concept of a niche is inaccurately thought of as being indefinable. Not many people are quite sure what a niche is. Is it simply a subsidiary market with special needs that can be served by special companies? Or is it actually a market that is too insignificant for the sector leaders to be interested in?

Since approximately 600,000 companies worldwide are affected by the subject of niche strategy, this topic should be a major concern as global consolidation occurs. However, this is clearly not the case. Even if Michael Porter were to raise the respectability level of a niche strategy, few researchers and strikingly few practitioners have considered the subject, and even Porter treats it as a carnival sideshow to the global three-ring circus.

In addition to many underestimates by business pundits, hardly any other group of strategies has misled business owners and managers in such a fatal way as an unsuccessful or unsuccessfully defended niche. Examples of illusory niche strategies are like sand castles by the sea.

ROLLS-ROYCE OUTGROWS ITS TARGET-GROUP NICHE

Rolls-Royce was established in 1906 by Charles Stewart Rolls and Frederick Henry Royce, who wanted to produce cars exclusively for the highest luxury class in an already widespread market within the automotive industry. Pursuing a product/target-group niche was an appropriate move, given that the automotive sector was just coming out of its Opening Phase and entering its Scale Phase. The founders enjoyed rapid success, and for many decades Rolls-Royce was the vehicle not only of members of royalty and popes, but also of dictators and leaders of the underworld. Old models are conserved today like museum pieces and brought out, cleaned, polished, and displayed for connoisseurs. After World War II, however, the company took a beating, as its target market—society's wealthy—was hit hard financially. Rolls-Royce clung mightily to its debilitated target-group niche and tottered on the brink of bankruptcy, which ultimately became its fate in 1971.

In that year, this traditional U.K. company was nationalized; after many ups and downs, it was acquired in 2003 by BMW. At the time, nothing remained of the automobile legend except the brand name, which still had broad value. Rolls-Royce's technology, which had been light-years ahead at the company's inception, had become four decades behind. Also in 2003, BMW brought out the Rolls-Royce Phantom. The new vehicle's interior integrated current BMW technology. BMW, a master target-group niche fighter, essentially found Rolls-Royce by the roadside and replaced the engine, hydraulics, tires, and suspension—everything except the Rolls-Royce look and name.

Did Rolls-Royce management make a fatal mistake? Not really. It just sold out 40 years too late. Or maybe management's mistakes did lead to Rolls-Royce's demise. If companies follow a niche strategy, even an Endgame niche strategy, their cash-out value should always be one of their key performance indicators. But Rolls-Royce exploited an early-phase Endgame niche—target group—and rode it far too long. The company provides a dignified, but rather sorry, example of the failure of niche strategies.

Staying in the automotive industry, let's look at another example—Porsche. Porsche was established in 1931 as a pure sports car supplier. In its first few years, the company achieved a brand name as strong as Rolls-Royce's, but only in the sports car market—again a good product/target-group niche strategy in the early Scale Phase of global automotive consolidation. In addition to producing its own cars, Porsche initially developed cars for the newly established Volkswagen group, and over the years it weathered crises similar to Rolls-Royce's. However, Porsche profited from a very stable owners' group whose members identified themselves with the company and the brand even in times of crisis. This was the beginning of Porsche's transformation from a target-group niche strategy to a branding/lifestyle niche strategy.

Since 1992, Porsche has achieved textbooklike success with an expansion strategy, a step-by-step approach that allowed the company to evolve from an initial, narrowly defined niche to a diversified product range. Porsche went from being purely a sports car supplier to producing other types of cars, including a four-seat sports limousine in the works. The company is changing from a niche supplier to a manufacturer with a broader product range and a powerful branding/lifestyle niche. Whether Porsche can maintain its current niche strategy as an independently owned company for the long term or will ultimately require a larger parent company or similar arrangement remains to be seen. The recent cross-holding with the Volkswagen group seems to point in the latter direction.

Niche companies are found not only in major industrial sectors but also in service industries. For example, the Swiss company Bon

Appétit, a medium-sized food retail supplier, provided mobile service units and its own regionally defined culinary service, concentrating on the target-group niche of "alpine villages." After a decade of successful growth and attractive profits, Bon Appétit came into the line of fire of large suppliers such as Migros, REWE, and the food-service wing of Nestlé, all of which were achieving advantages of scale and consolidating their suppliers. Within a few months, Bon Appétit was in a crisis situation; its assets were split among the global consolidators in 2004.

It is important to consider successful niche strategies in light of the Merger Endgame Theory, which asserts that every industry will consolidate globally over time. This is important not only for the executive managers of these companies, but also for the leadership of global consolidators such as Procter & Gamble and Nestlé, which need to understand when to buy these little gems, when to avoid them, and when to stand on the sidelines shaking their heads in sorry disbelief. Consolidators and niche fighters alike must also remember the following points:

- A company's claims and reality are two different things. Guaranteed survival and success in niche markets have been achieved only by a diminishing number of companies. The overwhelming majority of these companies has not survived—and will not survive. The Merger Endgame Theory posits that 90 percent of the companies in existence today will not be around in 25 years. The inexorable impact of borderless capital, people, communications, and logistics will wipe out most of the niches that were previously thought of as safe.

- Too many executives lull themselves and their companies into complacency or false confidence, which leads to fatal strategic blunders. The Merger Endgame Theory predicts that industry sectors will go through their consolidation life cycle in 25 years.

- The empirical relevance of the niche problem is immense. The large majority of companies will sooner or later succumb to the inexorable juggernaut of global consolidation. Just for the record, the authors of this book aren't particularly happy about this trend. But having studied the empirical evidence for the past 25 years, we can only advise our business clients to accept it as a matter of fact. As much as we may all love companies such as Ben & Jerry's, the fact is that everything is consolidating. Just as the big bang theory defines the physical forces in our universe today, so does the Merger Endgame Theory define global business. The 600,000 niche companies that exist today need to take notice.

- There is an inappropriate lack of business literature on this issue. Too many stories abound of Davids beating Goliaths, or of conglomerates sweeping away all the great small businesses in their path. The authors of this book do not claim a moral high ground on either side of the issue. For every niche fighter, there is a time to fight the game and a time to sell. For every global consolidator, there are hundreds—even thousands—of acquisition opportunities clamoring for attention. Global businesses require a stronger foundation on which to make their decisions.

Chapter Two | Where Did All the Good Niche Strategies Go?

If the development of an industry were tracked for 10 to 20 years—a period that is beyond the planning horizon of most CEOs or even more theoretical corporate strategists—the fate of niche players would be easily apparent. Industries that are critical for economic health, such as automotive, automotive supplier, retail, pharmaceutical, construction, construction supply, steel, chemical, and many others, have endured massive layoffs and consolidation. Niche companies vanished overnight without so much as a whimper.

The media may have deplored the loss of local manufacturing, and some may place the blame for it on sending domestic business offshore, but the truth is much more benign—and much more frightening. In all the above-mentioned industries, only a few major companies now dominate each one, and smaller suppliers have disappeared completely from the scene. Wal-Mart and outsourcing are not to blame; each industry sector has its own DNA that describes its Endgame. The paper industry will last for a long time because there are large assets that must be dealt with. Electronics retailers will go quickly, as the supplier market is dominated by only a few players and consumers like to buy online. But most niches are just eddies on the sandy shores of a fast-moving stream.

Even though it's an obvious example of industry consolidation, let's take a look at the automobile industry and identify the key drivers of niche success—and failure (see Figure 2-1). Ferrari, Maserati, Lamborghini, Aston Martin, Jaguar, Bugatti, Alfa Romeo, De Tomaso, and Rover—all legendary companies and world-renowned brands—are now mere badges on other companies' cars. These companies have survived only as parts of larger companies such as Fiat, Ford, or Volkswagen. Only the finance, R&D, and marketing resources of these major groups have made it possible for these sports car brands to develop further technologically. Highly visible sponsorships in the car-racing world are indicative of the strong identity of these high-end sports brands.

Some brands, such as De Tomaso, have received financing from the Middle East, but lacked the technological or R&D capabilities of the global heavy hitters (making theirs an innovation niche). Whether these innovation niches can survive consolidation (from 17 to 7 or 5) remains to be seen. However, there has never been too much patience for innovation niches in the automotive industry, as DeLorean, Wankel, and countless others have learned to their misfortune.

However, sports car companies need not undergo a very public collapse. Sometimes scale-driven major producers build on their

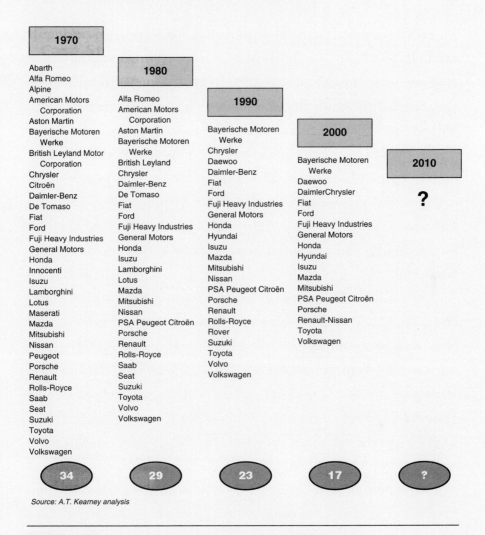

Figure 2-1. Concentration of the automobile industry, 1970 to 2010

capability to make "boring family cars" and add solutions for sports cars that are highly competitive. Good examples are Toyota, Honda, Renault, and many others. In 2005, Renault won the Formula One world championship against McLaren-Mercedes and Ferrari.

Steyr-Daimler-Puch is a particularly striking and tragic example of a failed niche strategy. The company saw itself as a multiniche supplier and had 10 product segments (trucks, tractors, ball bearings, handguns, buses, tanks, motorcycles, mopeds, bicycles, and people carriers), each of them apparently too small to survive and too large to collapse. These products were initially targeted for the Austrian market, which proved to be too small to avoid the consolidation of the global markets. Steyr-Daimler-Puch was aimed toward highly specialized niches (product, target-group, and regional) that were not defendable in the long term.

Not surprisingly, as the big boys duked it out at the grown-ups' table, the kids' table became substantially less populated too. The consolidation of the automobile electronics supply industry (as a representative of tier one and tier two auto suppliers) from 1970 to 1994 was profound, and has even accelerated since 1994 (see Figure 2-2).

The Merger Endgame Theory especially applies in the retail industry—which is important to all of us both as businesspeople and as human beings. As much as shoppers miss their Marshall Field's or Morrisons, consolidation isn't going to slow down anytime soon. When was the last time you visited your stand-alone butcher, fishmonger, delicatessen, hardware store, photo shop, bank, or cheese shop?

Independently owned retailers have now been integrated into supermarkets or large retail chains. Consolidation is also obviously accelerating given the economic turmoil of early 2008 in traditional department stores, which are increasingly losing market share in retail to big-box discounters. Although the "Wal-Mart effect" occurs

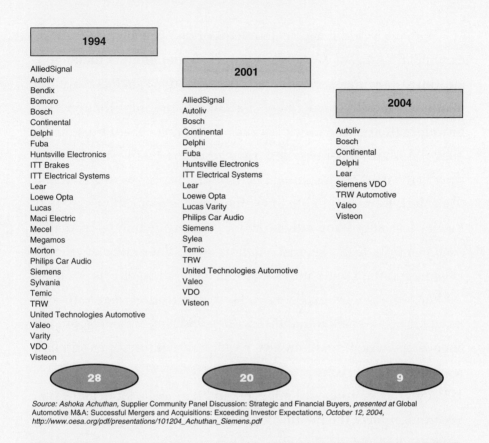

Source: Ashoka Achuthan, Supplier Community Panel Discussion: Strategic and Financial Buyers, *presented at* Global Automotive M&A: Successful Mergers and Acquisitions: Exceeding Investor Expectations, *October 12, 2004,* http://www.oesa.org/pdf/presentations/101204_Achuthan_Siemens.pdf

Figure 2-2. Concentration of automobile electronics manufacturers, 1994 to 2004

in the United States, and similar effects from Carrefour, Lidl, and Aldi have shaken up their respective markets, the real story is global. And that's why, although many customers accept these consolidations, some obviously don't. It's not just new formats and new assortments that throw consumers into upheaval. There is still strong brand franchise power, as Federated discovered when it removed Chicago's doughty Marshall Field's logo and replaced it with Macy's.

Without a doubt, the scale effects of giants such as Wal-Mart, Carrefour, Tesco, or Metro are so superior that product niche players, apart from those catering to a high-luxury segment, have little power to compete. Some blame Wal-Mart for forcing other retailers to reduce their already rock-bottom prices (a recent study estimated that Wal-Mart's low-price performance created a five-to-one economy in the market—meaning that other retailers, striving to be like Wal-Mart, were working to lower their prices too).

It's less surprising to hear about the consolidation of so-called commodity industry sectors, such as steel, flour milling, cement, paper, aluminum, and milk. The impact of scale effects occurred earlier and was more expected in these industries. However, to some extent, it was assumed that the effect would be felt more in product niches and target-group niches, particularly in the paper and milk industries.

A stellar example of both good and bad niche strategies is the reorganization of the pharmaceutical industry. The pharmaceutical industry had very clearly defined product niches that, because of the differences in the molecules involved, did not make any target-group or value-chain similarities very likely. Nevertheless, an industry consolidation has occurred and will continue for the next few years. Well-known global niche suppliers such as Merck, Schering, and Boehringer Mannheim, as well as the suppliers of over-the-counter medicines, are expected to be swallowed up by consolidation. As a matter of fact, as we prepared this book, it was quite difficult to keep current with examples of companies being consolidated, as more companies were evaporating with each rising sun. The pharmaceutical industry's consolidation was independent of its R&D and product niches, in which the individual generic manufacturers and small ethical drug suppliers have been operating. These players lost because they chose a specific niche at the wrong time. Those that survived did so because they chose the right Endgame niche strategy at the right time.

If you don't think Endgame niches have an impact on the national economy, consider what happened in the German banking sector. The banking industry in Germany, the public and federal banking sector in particular, was restructured. The private banks (those that had not already been acquired) initially offered an extensive range of services, but they began to concentrate on niche markets such as wealthy individuals. These companies could not match the economies of scale of the major banks, especially the aggressive foreign major banks. Private banks that have now been consolidated include Merck Finck & Co., Schröder Münchmeyer Hengst & Co., Aufhäuser, Bethmann, Hardy, BHF-BANK, Schmidt Bank, and Sloman. The story is very much the same in other national and regional markets. Each of the authors has experienced it directly. Our local Banque Hervet in Paris has been taken over by HSBC, and JPMorgan Chase has gobbled up First Chicago.

In case this discussion seems anecdotal, take a look at Figure 2-3, which displays the earnings capacity of banks against the degree of global consolidation—a powerful engine that drives the inexorable consolidation.

One of the things that stand in the way of the Merger Endgame Theory taking effect is noneconomic regulatory interference. Thirty years ago, there were many reasons why banks couldn't, shouldn't, or wouldn't be global. However, in this age of global capital, people, and communications, it is increasingly difficult to think of a reason why the banking industry should not have just three global

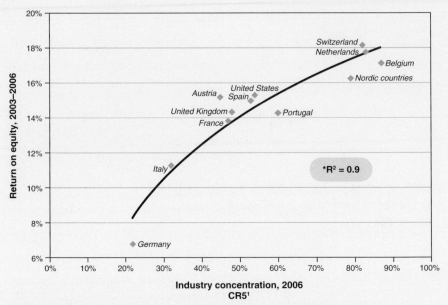

*R^2 is a statistical measure that evaluates the goodness of fit of a regression analysis. Values range between 0 and 1, and the higher the R^2, the more confidence one can have in the analysis (source: Barron's Educational Series, Inc.).
[1]CR5 = market share of the five largest companies of the total market based on the Value Building Growth database (660,000 companies).
Sources: Value Building Growth database; A.T. Kearney analysis

Figure 2-3. Correlation between concentration and earnings capacity for banks in national markets

leaders, plus a few niche fighters such as Cattles plc. It is entirely likely that in 25 years there will not be a single German-owned bank operating in Germany (or in France or even in England). The banking industry's DNA has already determined who will own the bank on your street.

Chapter Three | Know When to Hold 'Em . . .

The title of this chapter refers to the poker player's dilemma, captured in a Kenny Rogers song, of looking at an ugly hand of five-card stud and an uglier group of tablemates:

You got to know when to hold 'em
Know when to fold 'em
Know when to walk away
And know when to run

The business world is a volatile place where the big corporations are sometimes impossible to figure out and there is so much information overload in the smaller businesses that you can never be sure who's in the lead. That's the reason we put 98 percent of the world's economy through the wringer for the past 15 years: to let the data tell us what was happening—not what the *Economist* or the *Financial Times* or the *Wall Street Journal* thought was happening, but what was *actually* happening.

What we found was truly astounding. We did not find a random pattern from which we could not predict the future. Instead, the data revealed almost exactly what we had predicted in our previous six books on the subject, this being the first time we had focused on niche segments.

A deeper investigation into the 90 percent (600,000) of today's businesses that will be acquired or put out of business in the next 25 years in the consolidation frenzy compelled us to develop the theories in this book. This is all based on the Merger Endgame Theory, which is summarized here (see Figure 3-1).

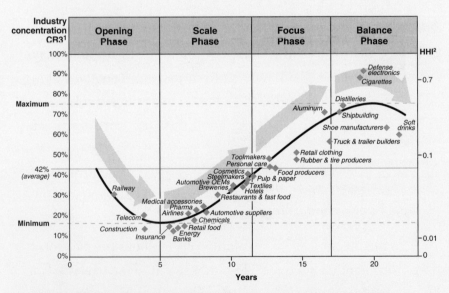

¹ CR3 = market share of the three largest companies of the total market based on the Value Building Growth database (660,000 companies).
² HHI = Hirschman-Herfindahl Index, which corresponds to the sum of the squared market shares of all companies and is greater than 90%; the axis is logarithmically plotted.
Sources: Value Building Growth database; A.T. Kearney analysis

Figure 3-1. Merger Endgame curve of industrial consolidation

On the basis of the Value Building Growth database, which contains information gathered on 660,000 companies worldwide (and 98 percent of world market capitalization) during a 15-year period, it is possible to identify the structural shifts that occur in each sector over time, explain them, and predict their future. Detailed Merger Endgame Theory analyses indicate that all industry sectors consolidate in a period of about 25 years. This happens in a clear series of phases. In the last phase, the Balance Phase, only three or four market leaders—or global consolidators—share the majority of the global market.

During the earlier Scale and Focus Phases, industry sectors reorganize the weaker suppliers; as a rule, these are always niche players. Therefore, niche suppliers, despite their efforts to avoid being swallowed up by market leaders, have clearly defined windows of opportunity for their existence. According to the results of the study, niche players are either bought out or shut down when this window closes. Alternatives do exist. Using one of the Endgame niche strategy models may enable a business to survive into the Balance Phase or even split off into a separate market and dominate it over time. If this alternative is not possible, the niche company can acknowledge its limited window of opportunity and determine the best time for it to be sold to one of the market leaders. A dramatic example of this is the premium price commanded by Alcan in its sale to Rio Tinto. After recognizing that the company's duel with Alcoa would not result in a global consolidator role, Alcan's leadership decided that its product niche strategy had run its course, and that maximizing shareholder value through the sale of the company was the best course of action. *Know when to fold 'em* (see Figure 3-2).

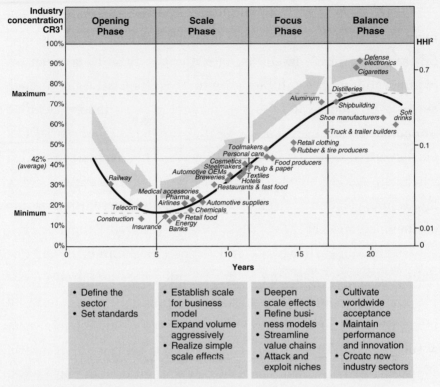

Figure 3-2. Merger Endgame phases and their strategic requirements

The study also showed that when market consolidation is imminent, aspiring market leaders in each Endgame phase should pursue clear strategies and operational missions to not only be successful but also achieve world market leadership. If a company cannot execute these strategies, it will sooner or later leave the market. According to the results of our analysis, niche players usually become the victims of consolidation during the Focus Phase. The optimum time for niche companies to consider being sold, therefore, is at the start of the Focus Phase.

Global consolidation is driven by scale effects, which increasingly put market leaders in a position to convert volume-driven unit-cost advantages into either price cuts or added performance features (without raising prices), therefore driving competitors out of the market. These scale effects are initially easy to understand. For example, in industries that produce mass goods, in which a company's products are clearly defined and fairly standardized, volume advantages can be enjoyed immediately. Examples are basic chemical companies, semimanufactured goods suppliers for the metals industry, and retail food chains. In these instances, volume advantages can be immediately converted into purchase-price advantages, increased productivity, and reduced fixed costs.

Similar advantages are even possible with highly specialized products. The difference is in the value chain, which, in the case of such products, is driven by the scale of the tier one and tier two suppliers. An example is the platform strategy used in automobile production, in which 80 to 85 percent of the value creation is clearly scale-driven, and the final 15 to 20 percent is represented by customization.

In addition to the scale advantages achieved through growth and acquisition, the Merger Endgame Theory analysis also provides deep insight into the profitability of the global consolidators in each phase of consolidation. This additional insight provides a better view of the "grow or die" mandate that drives consolidation from simple scale aggregation to further consolidation in the Focus Phase.

With a slight delay in time, the profit curve follows the Endgame curve (see Figure 3-3). In the Opening Phase, innovators and state-regulated industries enjoy high, sometimes very high, initial profits. With increasing fragmentation, these profits fall to a relative minimum, but then rise consistently with increased consolidation.

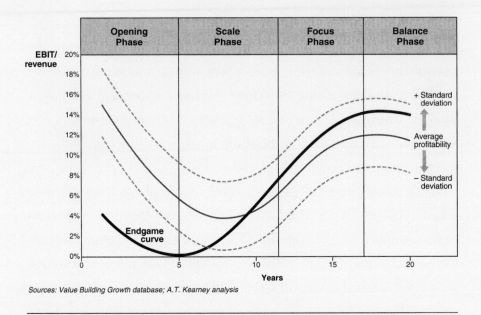

Figure 3-3. Profitability follows the Endgame curve

At the end of the Focus Phase, or the start of the Balance Phase at the latest, profits are at their peak. Industries with the highest degree of consolidation, and therefore the highest internal scale effects, logically show the highest profits. Accordingly, companies with the lowest scale effects achieve the lowest profits.

Private equity companies use the effects along the Endgame curve to target the timing of investments or divestitures. At the start of the Scale Phase, when an industry has achieved the highest degree of fragmentation and the companies' profits are low, many companies can be bought at low prices. These companies can then be sold at the turning point of the curve, about five to seven years later, when the market leaders that have slowly emerged are willing to pay top prices to capture additional market share and achieve further consolidation and growth.

As industries diversify, individual companies or industries find their strategic positions. During this phase of the Endgame curve, companies should map their revenue growth and value growth on the Value Building Growth matrix. Through this mapping, the positions of the companies in each industry sector can be identified. A company's position in the matrix shows the relationship it holds vis-à-vis its competitors, as well as its chances of success in surviving consolidation. This position on the Value Building Growth matrix makes it possible for that company to select the appropriate niche strategy and respond to the strategic profile of the market leaders.

The players in the automobile industry, as shown in Figure 3-4, are positioned on the basis of average revenue growth (vertically) and average value growth (horizontally). The size of the circles rep-

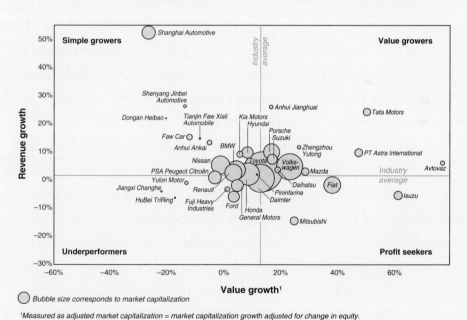

Figure 3-4. Value Building Growth scatter of the automobile industry

resents each player's market capitalization. Toyota is clearly dominant; its market capitalization is nearly as high as that of the rest of the global automobile industry. The upper right quadrant (which is called the value grower quadrant) shows those companies for which both revenues and value are growing more rapidly than the sector average. Here we find Porsche, along with new players such as Tata Motors and PT Astra International. BMW and Hyundai—historically in the value growers quadrant—have moved to the left in the last two years as the market penalizes them for their simple growth push. Clearly, mergers with some of the other suppliers will be necessary to reduce the gap with Toyota. The recent cross-holding of Porsche in Volkswagen is a move in this direction.

Volkswagen is in the upper right, or value grower, quadrant. The company shows above-average sales growth and is favored by the capital markets because of its "merger" with Porsche. General Motors and Ford are in the lower left, or underperformer, quadrant. Despite being global leaders in sales, they are valued by the market at one-sixth of Toyota's market capitalization. Years ago, the substantial risks facing these two former giants were made clear in our analysis, and the most recent news in the press continues to confirm this earlier finding.

Daimler—also in the underperformer quadrant—is also a solid candidate for a turnaround. Its earlier strategy of the "World AG," oriented toward achieving world market leadership, failed in the end as a result of completely inept implementation. The acquisition by Cerberus of the Chrysler assets puts Daimler back in a precarious position. As the course of the automobile-sector Endgame progresses, Daimler will probably not be able to carry on fighting alone.

There is potential for niche businesses in many areas, but at the start of the Focus Phase, the possibilities are limited. Product niches have run out, and innovation niches are harder to apply, as seen in the example; market leader Toyota is already significantly in the lead in the development of environmentally friendly and fuel-efficient cars. With branding/lifestyle niches, it remains to be seen whether Porsche or Ferrari will be able to maintain their positions of strong brand distinction. Cooperation niches are already apparent for many automakers. Creating and maintaining counter niches certainly require creativity, making these niches possible for only a few companies.

In another example, the pharmaceutical industry, the consolidation race is not yet over (see Figure 3-5). There is still a substantial struggle among Pfizer, GlaxoSmithKline, and Novartis (and possibly sanofi-aventis) for dominance in the Endgame. All others appear to be out of the race already.

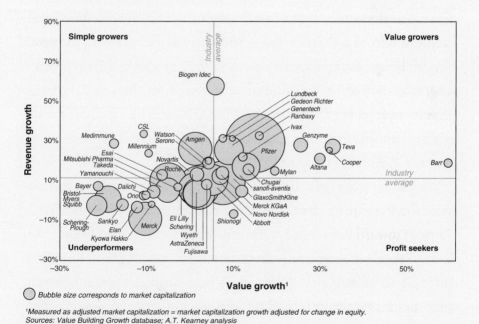

Bubble size corresponds to market capitalization

[1]Measured as adjusted market capitalization = market capitalization growth adjusted for change in equity.
Sources: Value Building Growth database; A.T. Kearney analysis

Figure 3-5. Value Building Growth scatter of the pharmaceutical industry

The pharmaceutical industry was previously segmented by distinct product offerings, with individual segment leaders holding strong niche positions. This segmentation is rapidly ending as the Endgame progresses, with the result that only global, scale-driven companies with strong R&D, multiproduct offerings, and strong sales are surviving. Germany was once the "pharmacist to the world." Market leaders such as Bayer, Hoechst, and Boehringer specialized in product niches, but these have either been consolidated or lost significant market share.

There has been a wave of biotech companies that first pursued an innovation niche, and then integrated with "old pharma" companies to exploit overall scale effects. This demonstrates how rapidly the Merger Endgame life cycle can churn through sectors, and how sector consolidation can create an economic engine in which niche fighters and global consolidators interact in an almost symbiotic relationship. The 2006 acquisition of Serono—a 100-year-old Swiss niche player—by Merck for $15.6 billion reinforces the inexorable nature of consolidation. Conversely, the entry of major pharmaceutical companies such as Novartis and Bayer into the market for generic molecules also clarifies the importance of scale effects for the global leaders.

Not surprisingly, if we map pharmaceutical industry companies on the Value Building Growth matrix, with innovation niche fighters and global consolidators together, the innovation niche fighters point in the direction of the value growers' neighborhood while industry stalwarts such as Bayer, Schering-Plough, and Merck point to the southwest in the underperformers' corner. This is not unlike the experience of the automotive sector (see Figure 3-6).

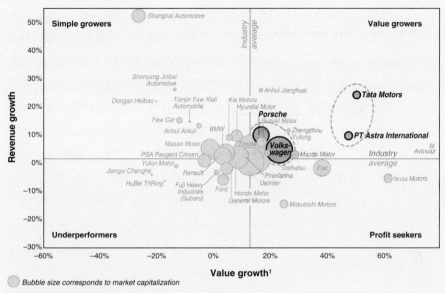

Bubble size corresponds to market capitalization

[1]Measured as adjusted market capitalization = market capitalization growth adjusted for change in equity.
Sources: Value Building Growth database; A.T. Kearney analysis

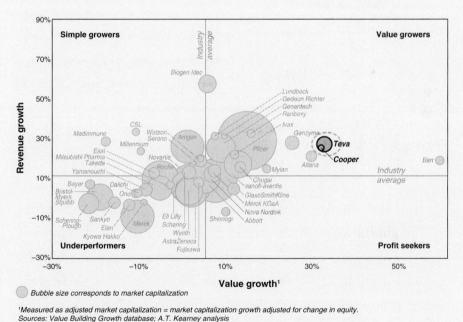

Bubble size corresponds to market capitalization

[1]Measured as adjusted market capitalization = market capitalization growth adjusted for change in equity.
Sources: Value Building Growth database; A.T. Kearney analysis

Figure 3-6. High-performing small businesses in the automobile industry (*top*) and the pharmaceutical industry (*bottom*)

As mentioned before, not only does the Merger Endgame Theory have high empirical relevance at the revenue level, but the EBIT/revenue performance curve—the "U curve"—is equally relevant across industry sectors. Consider the example shown in Figure 3-7 from the global adhesives industry.

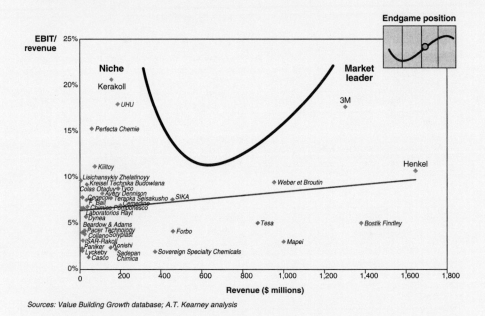

Sources: Value Building Growth database; A.T. Kearney analysis

Figure 3-7. Value Building Growth scatter of the adhesives industry

It is worth noting that the combined profitability of the niche fighters and the global leaders is greater than the combined profitability of all the companies in between; this applies across all industry sectors. The U-shaped curve that Michael Porter hypothesized in his 1980 book *Competitive Strategy* is substantiated by our empirical analysis of the 32,000 public companies in the Merger Endgame Theory model.

If we expand the analysis to all industry sectors and look at the 32,000 publicly traded companies, we can see that the U curve (see Figure 3-8), while not so pronounced as it is in the adhesives sector, still supports the Merger Endgame Theory shown in Figure 3-3.

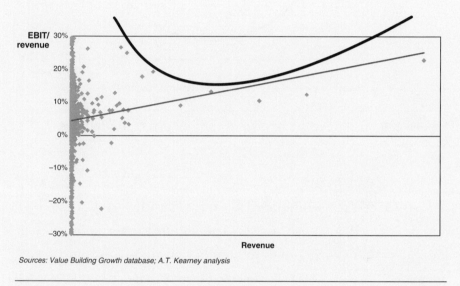

Sources: Value Building Growth database; A.T. Kearney analysis

Figure 3-8. U-shaped curve of the 32,000 publicly traded companies

Figure 3-9 shows the profit advantage of market leaders and global consolidators, but also, as Porter puts it, of the "differentiators" or niche fighters.

But let's take Porter's theorem and put a little more rigor into the analysis. If we take the four phases of the Merger Endgame Theory—Opening, Scale, Focus, and Balance—and divide each of these phases into four subphases ranging from "early" to "late," we can map the niche players in each of the 16 resulting phases of the

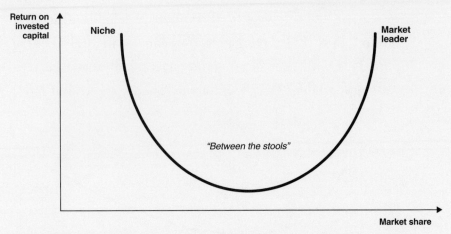

Source: Michael E. Porter, Competitive Strategy: Techniques for Analyzing Industries and Competitors (New York: Free Press, 1980)

Figure 3-9. U-shaped curve diagram from Porter, *Competitive Strategy*

industry sector consolidation. This almost results in a year-by-year account of an industry sector's consolidation. The result is striking, but not entirely surprising: the number of high-performing small companies declines with increasing consolidation. The niche population becomes disproportionately smaller until the market leaders eventually dominate (see Figure 3-10). However, it is important to note that although there are fewer niche opportunities as the Merger Endgame life cycle progresses, *there are still niche survivors in every phase*.

We discussed earlier why there are large numbers of niche players in the Scale and Focus Phases, which is shown empirically in Figure 3-10. As the Merger Endgame Theory has shown, with the right moves, specific niche strategies can survive within certain windows of opportunity and achieve high profitability alongside the scale leaders, even in the long term.

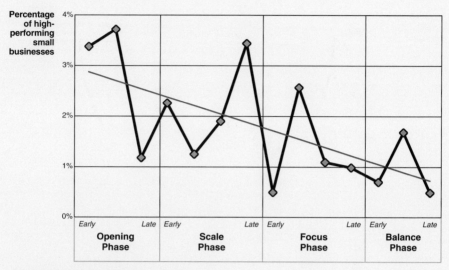

Note: There are 0 companies in subphases 1 and 16.
Sources: Value Building Growth database; A.T. Kearney analysis

Figure 3-10. The percentage of high-performing small businesses declines as industries consolidate

Niches Are Born, Live, and Die within Larger Markets

At a presentation to the A.T. Kearney European Chief Procurement Officer (CPO) Club in Rome on the subject of "Consolidating Industries and Their Impact on Procurement," in which there was also a discussion about the ultimate fate of niches, the purchasing head of a leading Spanish bank mentioned that, in his language, the origins of the word *niche* were derived from "burial chamber." Because of a shortage of space, these burial chambers were normally found carved out of walls beneath the earth.

It's not a very pleasant association, but the anecdote is notable. No other word inspires as much confusion as *niche*, particularly in a strategic context. The range of meanings is reflected in comments that emphasize how good niches are, as in the frequently heard remark that "all German mid-cap companies are niche suppliers;

that's why they're so profitable," and comments that emphasize their evanescence, as in "market niches become smaller and smaller in the course of consolidation until they leave the market." Even the often-cited "hidden champions" are described as niche suppliers to some extent, although upon closer inspection they consist primarily of companies that have an extremely high market share in a small yet independent market. This leads to correspondingly strong competitive positions and profitability. It is almost impossible for other players to threaten these strong positions until regional barriers to entry are no longer protective.

We agree with the consensus of other business strategists (Kotler, Kröber-Riehl, Cavalloni, and Porter) that a niche market can be defined as a "partial market," or part of a larger market. A market is defined as a combination of supply and demand for a specific good or service. A partial market in this context is a segment of a market that, in theory, can be served by all suppliers equally. However, these partial markets make it possible for individual suppliers to focus on specific segments. The following characteristics apply to niche companies:

- The niche is formed or created by the company in relation to the market environment.
- The underlying overall market is a critical reference, and the niche should be considered in connection with it.
- The niche is small in comparison to the market as a whole. However, it still achieves an adequate sales volume to justify its unique approach and enjoys relevant and appropriate economies of scale.
- Successful niche suppliers use specialization and focus on the niche to create growth platforms.

■ Dissatisfied clients play an important role in the creation and growth of niches. Niches have a protected position in some cases, which creates barriers to entry for other competitors.

While these definitions and characteristics are valid in a stable environment, they rapidly run aground in a dynamic consolidation environment and as markets evolve, which we discuss in the following section. Our deeper analysis of the dynamics of consolidation and market segment evolution provides an opportunity to frame the entire discussion of niche strategy in a new light and will help provide a more in-depth understanding than has been available in the literature up to this point.

Markets evolve in response to many influences, such as customer requirements, competitor capabilities, and financial and regulatory incentives and restrictions. Technology and innovation, however, drive most of the moves into various subsidiary markets (see Figure 4-1).

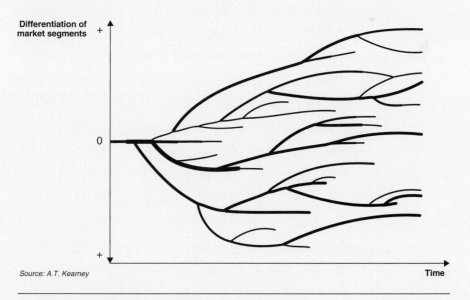

Source: A.T. Kearney

Figure 4-1. Evolution of niche markets

The information technology (IT) sector is a good example of the nature of market evolution. When the computer industry first originated, the first priority was to produce and sell computers that provided users with the capacity for computation and storage of data. Like steam engines a century earlier, the first computers were big, centrally managed affairs. The frisson that swept through the user community with remote job entry (RJE) in the 1970s is illustrative of how incredibly clunky computers were then—and how one-dimensional the user experience was. RJE meant that you could lug your box of IBM punch cards to a location different from the computer's and still run your job. But even the concept of "lugging a box of cards" is so foreign to the current perception of the computation, communication, and storage environment that the IT sector might as well have been communicating by smoke signals in the 1970s. The industry was dominated by "my way or the highway" types such as IBM until the late 1970s and companies such as Siemens, UNIVAC, Sperry, Bull, Fujitsu, Nixdorf, and Olivetti were far behind in the course of consolidation.

A variety of factors drove the evolution of the computer industry: customer requirements for more decentralized computing and data storage capabilities; specialization into components, assembly, and modular software system design; the leveraging of assets to provide on-demand IT services; and many others. As businesses realized that information could be a substitute for *everything*—inventory, assets, people—value chains were recreated on an almost weekly basis. In response to these pressures, the market diversified into segments such as software, hardware, and services. Each segment formed its own new market, followed by the creation of even further subdivisions. In the Opening Phase of the Endgame, all of the players operated in one market with one Endgame scenario. As the market diversified, each new subsidiary market sector created its own unique Endgame (see Figure 4-2).

Not all markets branch and diversify in the same way as the computer industry. The automobile industry, for example, experienced market convergence when various automobile markets—regional markets, supplier markets for subsystems, consumer segments for model types—actually grew together as a result of technological integration and overlaps in the value chain. However, most industries—including chemicals, pharmaceuticals, electronics, and machine tools—have evolved by branching and diversify-

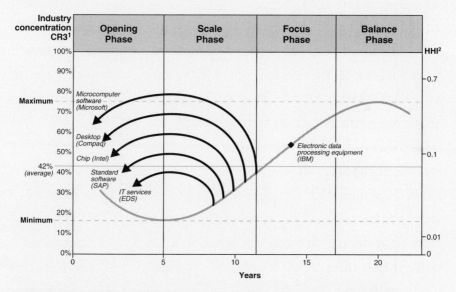

[1] CR3 = market share of the three largest companies of the total market based on the Value Building Growth database (660,000 companies).
[2] HHI = Hirschman-Herfindahl Index, which corresponds to the sum of the squared market shares of all companies and is greater than 90%; the axis is logarithmically plotted.
Sources: Value Building Growth database; A.T. Kearney analysis

Figure 4-2. Market splitting of the IT industry through the Endgame curve

ing. These industries have also spawned relatively more numerous niche fighters in their Endgame life cycle.

The findings from this discussion of market evolution will be discussed later in the book as we formulate practical approaches for identifying and implementing successful Endgame niche strategies. But first, let's look at the universe of niche players in the overall context.

Chapter Five | Small Is Beautiful, but It Can Be Pretty Big Too

The niche phenomenon is extremely significant, and in sheer numbers, niches are among today's most strategic issues. We have alluded to this before, but we will now dive in with more detail. Successful Endgame niche fighters not only can rebuff unwelcome advances from the global consolidators, but also can develop the power to confront and in some cases even overwhelm them.

In every industry, small and medium-sized players obviously outnumber the leaders. As we have shown, every industry goes through the Merger Endgame life cycle. At the end of the Opening Phase, the number of businesses in each industry sector is higher than it will ever be again. Then about 90 to 95 percent of these businesses are lost in the Scale and Focus Phases and never reach the Balance Phase.

According to the results of our empirical analysis, every global industry sector consolidates within a 25-year period. Every company, at any time, is capable of being an Endgame niche winner or loser. The question for all of these businesses is: What is the best Endgame niche strategy? And the next question is: Will this require a fundamental shift in strategy? To decide where they will enter the game, niche "players" and niche "fighters" (and you have probably already discerned the distinction between these two terms— niche fighters will rebuff unwelcome advances) must ask themselves the following questions:

- How should I attempt to influence the market to form a subsidiary market of my own that I can dominate? What are my customers' dissatisfactions? What are their unknown desires? More importantly, what's going on in China, Slovenia, the Philippines, Indonesia, Ukraine, or Iran that I should know about? If I have success as a regional niche fighter, perhaps there are other customers in other regions who have similar interests.

- How do I position myself in the market segments with the most growth potential? This relates strongly to the scale issue. In the late 1990s, despite warning signals that were ablaze at every point in the journey, a lot of smart people placed a lot of big bets against the future of brick-and-mortar retailers, and yet they didn't go away—at least not to the extent that anybody thought they would. Sometimes the answer to the question isn't where you expect it.

- How do I focus on a subsidiary market that is less vulnerable to consolidation? This is the core question. While the global consolidators are pursuing the economic logic of the past 50 years, everyone else is scrambling to create a product, serve a client, meet a need, or fulfill a dream. Our research brushes off the fuzzy thinking on this question. We address it in the next few chapters.

■ How can I survive as long as possible against competitive pressure? How long should I stay in business before selling the company to maximize its lifetime value? Without a doubt, the most powerful recommendations from the Merger Endgame Theory and this deeper analysis of successful Endgame niches is that the leadership team of each of the 600,000 niche players must evaluate the firm's disposition value as clearly and as dispassionately as it does its days' sales outstanding and accounts receivable balance. In addition, many niche players are family-held businesses—which puts a huge roadblock in the journey toward dispassionate strategic thinking. Later in this book, we discuss how family pride can stand in the way of good economic judgment.

Despite the emotional and human aspects of these questions, our empirical research of the past 25 years exposes the factors that undermine the best intentions of management. We see how customers in the commercial marketplace—who determine revenue growth—interpret management's strategies and, more important, its actions.

Perhaps when Hermann Simon's book *The Hidden Champions* became a bestseller in the 1990s, this was a big boost for a lot of so-called niche players in Germany. The majority of the small and medium-sized German companies featured in the book were among the 20 percent of such companies that are scale leaders in small markets. It follows that 80 percent of small and medium-sized

German companies are niche players that are in more or less strong competitive situations against their sector's leaders. Given that this group accounts for 49 percent of Germany's GDP and 70 percent of all jobs, the subject of niche businesses is a central topic for German macroeconomics, even though researchers have not actually acknowledged it as such. The fact that a large number of niche companies are successful in Germany is unquestionable. However, the Merger Endgame Theory strongly suggests that most of these businesses will not fare well in the Endgame, however healthy they are today.

The rest of the developed markets in Europe, Asia, and North and South America have generally similar structures.

THE ENTIRE SOUTHERN AND EASTERN EUROPEAN REGION IS A NICHE MARKET

If niches account for a large part of the viability of a developed economy such as Germany's, how important are they to developing markets? A quick glance at Eastern Europe leads to the conclusion that the entire Eastern European region is a niche market. Until 1990, there were 4,000 Eastern European companies that had been established in the Council for Mutual Economic Assistance (COMECON) economic system and were initially in protected or monopoly positions. When Eastern European markets opened up, these established companies were exposed to competition from the already highly consolidated global market leaders in the West. They got caught in the current of global consolidation too rapidly and couldn't compete on qualitative terms, nor could they enjoy the scale effects that were already developed in the West. The bankruptcies of former state companies in eastern Germany that we have recently observed are only a precursor of further collapses yet to come in other Eastern European countries.

But East German companies had an extra burden to carry in the form of insurmountable debt. Large debt loads were not a problem when German debt was backed by the state, but in the postunification period, the currency conversion rate became a consumer-friendly ratio of 1:1. These companies were also hit with another consumer-friendly benefit: the West German salary system. The trade unions negotiated across-the-board salary agreements that gave entry-level employees two-thirds of West German salaries, even though productivity in the East was about 40 percent of that in the West. After being hit with these two disadvantages, hardly a single East German company has survived.

Companies in Poland, Hungary, the Czech Republic, Slovenia, Serbia, and Russia, on the other hand, usually had inflationary currencies and low salaries (10 to 30 percent of Western European levels). This initially offset the disadvantages of competing against Western European companies. However, the low cost of labor in these countries is already rising (though not as fast as consumer prices, which creates tension), and it will be difficult for these players to survive without dramatic improvements in their scale advantage.

NEW START-UPS IN CHINA AND INDIA—NICHES ON THE WAY TO THE TOP OF THE WORLD

Start-ups in China and India are in a much stronger position. The cost of labor in these regions is lower than in Eastern Europe, and economic planners in both countries recognize that the terms *global* and *scale* are the cornerstones of future success. China, in particular, has many government incentives to create industry winners in many sectors. For example, the retail giant Bailian Group was created through aggressive merger and joint venture activities with government planning and support. The company is now a $12 billion fighter—not necessarily big enough to win on size, but big enough to fight.

According to current data, there are a combined total of approximately 2,000 publicly held companies in China and India, and some of these are increasingly well positioned to move from a stable regional niche to a market leader or global consolidator. In the appliance sector, for example, Chinese producer Haier has generated revenues of more than $15 billion and is currently (with government support) penetrating the Western market. PetroChina's market cap is more than $1 trillion, which should give it some pretty strong hands to shape the Endgame in its sector. But it won't be easy: China National Offshore Oil Corporation's (CNOOC) bid for Unocal was met (and killed) with blatant xenophobia.

In the pharmaceutical industry, India's Ranbaxy is leveraging not only its cost-of-labor advantage but also the innovativeness of its R&D staff to give even the global leaders a run for their money.

China and India aren't wild cards in the global Endgame; they're a fifth and sixth suit in the deck of cards.

Chapter Six | How to Find and Nurture a Stable, Defendable, and Profitable Niche

By simple definition, niche players concentrate on subsidiary markets to avoid or at least mitigate direct competition with the scale-advantaged global market leaders. With the proper niche strategy, companies can escape consolidation—for a while—and enjoy a profitable business. We call these companies niche fighters. What are the foundations of a stable, defendable, and profitable niche? How can businesses create a successful niche strategy (or at least know when one is found)? And what can businesses do to keep running as long as possible? The three elements that make up an Endgame niche are shown in Figure 6-1.

1. *Segmentation.* Specialty market segments allow niche companies to play in the global business arena. Global leaders cannot both pursue a juggernaut strategy and address the specialized needs of every customer segment. The market

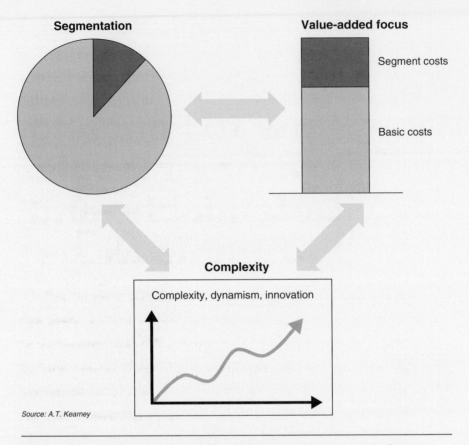

Figure 6-1. There are three elements that make up an Endgame niche: segmentation, value-added focus, and complexity

leaders all give lip service to providing customized products and services, catering to geographic and market differences, and addressing the needs of different buying behaviors; however, the truth is, their main priority is their own bottom line. This is not an editorial comment, but economic reality. If companies did not take this approach, shareholders would not buy their stock, their weighted average cost of capital would rise, and they would lose their competitiveness and fall victim to another industry leader that was more than happy to take the business. There is an upside in all this for niche fighters, however. Since the consolidators are almost exclusively fixated on the bottom line, this opens opportunities for smaller companies to come in and sweep up unserved needs that fall behind in the process—as long as they make the right moves.

2. *Value-added focus.* The second element of an Endgame niche is that niche players must focus on an area of the value chain different from that addressed by the market leader. This allows the niche fighter to win by capitalizing on a business opportunity in which the scale leader not only has little interest, but also has less capability to exploit the scale advantages it enjoys elsewhere. Here, the difference between the mainstream market and the niche market is particularly relevant and becomes an obvious Endgame niche market opportunity. If we differentiate between basic costs and segment costs in the value chain and compare an Endgame niche fighter with a scale leader, it is clear that the niche fighter has a higher share of segment costs. These costs must be proportionately high, so as to provide a barrier to scale leaders that seek to arbitrage their lower basic costs.

3. *Complexity.* The third element of an Endgame niche is that fighters must be dynamic and innovative. This requires not only mastering the skills of specialization and market focus, but also finally (in the context of the Merger Endgame Theory) being able to differentiate themselves from the scale leaders, which leads to more complexity. This ability is built on the skills described in the earlier phases of the Endgame,

but is enriched and empowered by a distinct personality. Sometimes this personality is embodied in a person, such as Steve Jobs or Richard Branson, who makes it a personal mission to expose the failings of the scale leaders. But more often than not it is a culture nurtured for years that attracts the type of employees who continue to wage war against global consolidation.

Every scale leader has weaknesses. A global consolidator can take advantage of its substantial scale effects to produce and offer a product inexpensively; however, this product obviously will not have the features expected of an Endgame niche product. In the early stages of sector consolidation, when the scale leader is scurrying to amass the market through the sheer volume of its acquisitions, or later, when the scale leader is struggling to digest its acquisitions into a portfolio that the market responds to, a niche product probably won't attract much attention. To seize the Endgame niche fighter's captured market, the scale leader knows that it would have to take on the associated segment costs. Later on in the sector consolidation process, a smart and innovative scale leader can, segment by segment, take out niche players that know only how to segment, specialize, and focus. To avoid this, Endgame niche fighters must strive to maintain their distinct personalities.

Technological innovation challenges scale leaders and Endgame niche players alike. However, the relatively large investment that global consolidators made to achieve their scale advantages often prevents them from exploiting the advantages that technological innovation brings, and the basic cost disadvantages of the Endgame niche players often stymie their efforts to jump ahead. During the next decade or two, the nature and pace of the technology revolution will keep all parties on their toes. It is not exactly clear how the winners will make trade-offs between agility and freedom and scale.

SEGMENT FOCUS: A NATURAL BARRIER TO MARKET LEADERS

The first segment on which niche players often focus is regional. If logistics have a strong impact on the cost of the finished product, market leaders often avoid certain regions. This opens up opportunities for niche players. These niche players can then establish themselves locally and serve the consumers close at hand. Scale leaders can play this game, too, but they cannot fully exploit their scale effects. For example, for decades Hindustan Lever has served the Indian market with quite a bit of independence. Most Indian consumers think of it as one of the better-known *local* companies, despite the fact that it is primarily owned by global consolidator Unilever. This company has only recently begun to truly exploit the scale effects of its parent—including changing its name to Hindustan Unilever in 2007—from which it will certainly benefit in the coming years.

Besides regional niches, there are as many other niches as there are ways to segment a market, whether it's by product, package, service, market, or behavior. If you can think of a dozen people who would spend a little more for something that's a little different, then that's the beginning of a niche. The more you can expand the segment, differentiate the value chain, and instill the niche with complexity, the more stable the niche becomes. A stable Endgame niche will survive until the middle of the Focus Phase, the third phase of the Merger Endgame Theory life-cycle curve.

Certain Endgame niches (regional, target group, and product) are not a one-way street to extinction, contrary to what is often asserted in economic theory. Indeed, they can reshape the sector and redefine what "scale leader" means. Wal-Mart, one of the most well-known scale leaders, was founded in 1962 with a mission to serve the "small-city consumer market," unlike other companies, such as Macy's and Marshall Field's, which were serving major urban markets at the time. Anyone standing in the sweltering parking lot in Bentonville, Arkansas, on the first opening day, with the foul-smelling ride-a-donkeys, the watermelons exploding in the heat, and the children crying, could not have imagined that this Endgame niche fighter would go on to redefine what retail meant to the U.S., and then the global, consumer. Part of the answer is timing. Wal-Mart started up at a time in which established urban and suburban centers were undergoing profound changes; this occurred again in the 1980s (during the upward flex of Wal-Mart's geometric growth curve), when technology fundamentally changed the value chain for retailers. Though it took several tries, Wal-Mart simply "got it" and went on to redefine not only retail but also what it means to be a scale leader in most consumer sectors.

How can companies identify and sustain an Endgame niche and stave off the acquisitive or destructive interests of the scale leader? The first step is to define a solid market segment. The second is to make the entry costs of challenging that segment so high that the scale leader and others look elsewhere.

A very sustainable segment is certainly the low-price segment, which has been at the core of new and extremely successful companies such as IKEA, ALDI, and H&M. IKEA, for example, extended its success in this segment by redefining its product range and image to make low prices synonymous with youth culture in a positive way.

Because the furniture market had a large number of distribution layers, making the value chain long and complex, IKEA revolutionized it by replacing the cost of logistics and inventory with added function and style. After the Second World War, young customers began to leave their parents' homes earlier than before and purchased their own homes instead of renting. IKEA rapidly became a hit with customers in Europe, not only because of the low price points, but also because of the high price-to-performance ratio. IKEA simply democratized the furniture market, and it is now one of the largest global brands. It is not surprising that IKEA's "Billy" shelf is a cult classic, found not only in student dorms but also in the library of Germany's former Chancellor Helmut Schmidt, who must certainly be in a higher income bracket. IKEA continues to track and attract its target group, and now caters to young families by adding high-quality food-service and child-care facilities to its stores; these customers, in return, reward IKEA with an average visit of more than two hours.

Finding a good specialization Endgame niche (regional, target group, or product) is like finding diamonds in the rough: if you have the right tools, you can carve a successful business that will keep you busy for years.

THE VALUE-CREATION FOCUS: NOW YOU HAVE TO BE AGILE, TOO

As previously discussed, market-leader economics and niche-fighter economics are fundamentally different. Market leaders invest a lot of time in whittling down their basic costs so that they can serve their markets with a widely accepted product range. They go out of their way to avoid segment-specific costs, but they cannot always do this without narrowing their range too drastically. Niche fighters spend a lot of time placing bets on segment investments that will allow them to serve their narrower markets with specialized and highly profitable product ranges. They go out of their way to avoid basic costs, but they cannot always do so because of their smaller scale.

The value-creation focus and the Endgame niches it generates (branding/lifestyle, speed/lightning consolidation, and innovation) require constant maintenance. Nothing stays the same, even for a day. The economics are similar to those of the specialization niches generated early in the Endgame life cycle, when the scale leaders are busy gobbling up all the others. But by the middle of the Focus Phase, these leaders are making strategic investments to rationalize and streamline their own portfolios by selling brands that don't fit and buying brands that do. In essence, they are changing their own value chain and the value chains of all the sector players on a weekly or daily basis. A good example of an industry in this phase is steel. Beginning in 2004, when Mittal Steel decided to pursue a lightning-consolidation Endgame niche strategy, every day was a new chapter in the industry's Endgame, whether it was a new headline or a new acquisition.

Niche players with a value-creation focus are strongly oriented toward a customer's immediate requirements. Therefore, they have a more complex value chain and cannot enter the low-priced segment, which is where the scale leaders dwell, converting production scale advantage into selling price advantage. In both the aluminum and the steel industries, market leaders that focused on pigs and ingots and tonnage were overthrown by niche fighters that emphasized more value-added products (Alcan in aluminum, Japanese producers in steel). This created a much more complex value chain, to be sure, but one that was well suited to satisfy the emerging segment of the steel- and aluminum-intensive downstream industries that were trying to outsource some of their own complexity.

The segment and basic costs of the value-creation process aren't the only factors that define a niche. Niches are also defined by how well the market leaders are performing. The less effectively the leaders are turning their scale advantages into sales volume, the larger and more stable the Endgame niches are. The more slowly the consolidators take advantage of or respond to value-chain differences, the longer the Endgame niches last. It is quite easy to assess a sector leader's effectiveness and speed to determine how robust the sector niches will be.

COMPLEXITY/DYNAMICS/INNOVATION: SYMBIOTIC RELATIONSHIPS IN THE SECTOR

The structural differences between the scale leader's and the Endgame niche player's value chains are revealed throughout a sector's life cycle. In the same way, "freedom" Endgame niches (innovation, cooperation, and market splitting) rely on the inflexibility of the scale leaders in reacting not only to Endgame niche players, but also to changes in the market. Scale leaders in the Balance Phase of the Merger Endgame Theory life cycle create and maintain their own markets, and create an algorithm that serves that market efficiently.

Complexity

Complexity is poison to a scale leader. Even if the company is large and its volume allows economies of scale, these advantages can be realized only if it is possible to reduce complexity. Whenever markets break up into segments, whether it's to serve various customer groups or to offer different product requirements or value-added models, it is hard for scale suppliers to respond. This allows the niche players some measure of protection against the giants for years, even decades. However, in certain sectors, the scale leader is able to deal with complexity in-house and pass on the economies of its innovation to the marketplace.

For example, the Volkswagen Group's platform strategy and modular production method are effective and cost-efficient ways to combine volume production with diverse market requirements. Not all sectors permit such an approach, and this creates more opportunities for Endgame niche strategies.

Dynamics

Dynamics refers to the speed and magnitude with which a sector responds to unexpected market upheavals. The greater the dynamics, the greater the opportunity for Endgame niche fighters to identify, nurture, and sustain an Endgame niche. Dynamic sectors are those with a high degree of innovation, such as biotechnology. However, even in a century-old sector such as telecommunications, the speed and magnitude with which the players respond to unexpected market upheavals is significant. A highly dynamic business environment is much like the fluctuating stock market: it diminishes the value of consolidation and increases the value of diversity.

Innovation

Innovation is the third element that offsets scale-leader advantages and opens up opportunities for Endgame niche players. Sector scale leaders must sail between Scylla and Charybdis: either they respond to the market with meaningful differentiation, or they deal with the complexity created by innovation. As we have mentioned earlier, scale leaders don't do well with complexity. Therefore, innovation is often left to the upstarts, which either become Endgame niche fighters or innovate themselves out of business (think of the biotech industry). We hear about only the successful ones. Scale leaders don't need that kind of stress. Innovation that leads to new products or completely new product characteristics accelerates the pressure on scale leaders, and as a rule these lumbering giants find it difficult to follow one dynamic change after another as the market segments.

There are exceptions. Some scale leaders, such as various units within Siemens and divisions of General Electric, quite deliberately develop their own counter strategies or cooperative agreements in which they work with smaller companies. They take these companies into their portfolio and experiment with them to generate innovation. Of course, the competitive opportunity for Siemens really starts as soon as the innovation loses its novelty value, the market calms down, and more constant and predictable demand sets in. Then the scale leader takes over the product and can start to achieve scale effects. Another great example is (was!) Gillette, a company that would bet 18 months of gross earnings on a new product launch, then, when market acceptance of the new innovation stabilized, integrate the new product into a manufacturing process that was so scale-oriented that it could have been outsourced, were it not for the trade secrets embedded in the product.

Without being able to mitigate the risk of innovation, niche players succeed or fail strictly on the economic success of their innovation. But the more successful the innovation, the more attention their niche will attract. Some companies acknowledge this and structure their activities accordingly. The Wm. Wrigley Jr. Company produces and markets some of the most stable brands in the universe—products that rely on scale effects to bring their selling price into an acceptable range for every five-year-old with pocket change. But Wrigley also runs a sister company called Amurol that is responsible for all the unusual confectionery products on the shelf that children crave: gum in the shape of guitars, squeezable gum in a tube, tiny gum, gum that crackles when you chew it, and more. Amurol creates products that, by design, have a short life cycle. By now, you can probably guess how the economics of Wrigley and Amurol are different.

INTERNATIONAL BUSINESS MACHINES: THE POSTER CHILD FOR BELEAGUERED SCALE LEADERS

The computer industry seemed well into the Balance Phase when Danny Kaye starred in *The Man from the Diners' Club* in 1963. However, starting around 1980, the industry was hit with wave after wave of complexity, dynamics, and innovation. At the start of the PC age in the late 1970s, the industry was dominated by the overall world market leader IBM, which had a global market share of almost 70 percent. The market began to evolve and segment (in a way that was almost parallel to the steam engine sector 100 or so years earlier) away from mainframes to more distributed computing power in the form of desktops and laptops. Because of its scale, IBM was well suited to serve this market for smaller machines, but it decided not to do so in order to protect its core business. This is a familiar scale-leader response to unexpected market upheaval. As a result, this new market was shaped by Compaq, Dell, Digital Equipment, Hewlett-Packard, and Fujitsu Siemens.

IBM also decided not to develop standardized software for many of the same reasons. Customers had favored individualized software in the industry's early years, which suited IBM's specialized, proprietary business model. This led to software spin-offs, created by companies such as SAP and Oracle, which then developed more standardized software in constantly expanding software sectors. The software industry achieved a market capitalization of well over $1 trillion—more than $315 billion of which is accounted for by Microsoft alone, whereas IBM captured less than $135 billion. Both desktop and software product groups were also originally part of IBM's value chain. Segments of the value chain branched out and new, independent industry sectors were created because of IBM's inflexibility in responding to changes in the market.

Outsourced computer services developed in a similar way. One example is Electronic Data Systems (EDS), which offered mainframe systems operation as a service. It merely modified the service component of mainframe systems, which had been sold to IBM customers who could afford the asset in one bite but was beyond the grasp of smaller or capital-strapped clients—something that IBM was not willing to explore.

In all of these developments, the Endgame niche fighters profited from the inflexibility of the market leader and its incapacity to respond to rapid market developments. Was IBM weak? No. In many ways it was too strong. Was IBM ignorant? Not really. It was tending its market very well. What was IBM's failing? The company was a global market leader—until Endgame niche fighters redefined its industry.

To its credit, IBM has found new life in the complexity, dynamics, and innovation of the new industry it finds itself in with a new portfolio: Business Services, Technology Services, IBM Software, and . . . what's the fourth one? Oh, right! *IBM Systems*.

We have taken you through a trip along the entire Merger Endgame Theory life-cycle curve, starting with the Opening Phase, through the Scale and Focus Phases, to the Balance Phase—a journey of 25 years in a few pages. Along the way we have demonstrated the three elements that make for a stable, defendable, and profitable Endgame niche: segmentation, value-creation focus, and complexity.

We have already shown that these three elements can play out in numerous ways. To see how they can be woven together to create success, you need look no further than the inhabitants of the upper right quadrant of the Value Building Growth matrix. These companies beat their sector average not only in sales growth, but also in market-cap growth from 1990 to 2006. As predicted, there are hundreds of them. From their experiences, we have identified nine Endgame niche strategies that work. They are profitable and they last, but they require constant nurturing to flourish as long as possible.

Chapter Seven | Nine Endgame Niches

The three elements of successful Endgame niches that were discussed in Chapter 6 appear in different manifestations along the Endgame life-cycle curve. In addition, the following overlaps usually occur:

- Market segmentation requires specialization.
- Value-chain differentiation requires focus.
- Complexity/dynamism/innovation requires agility.

The nine Endgame niches are archetypes, and are not often found in their pure form. They combine in a number of different ways—some more common, some quite rare—to create stable Endgame niche strategies. The combinations are in response to the different nature and structure of each industry sector, and our empirical analysis allows us to disaggregate them, which we will proceed to do here.

It is important to emphasize that in every industry sector, Endgame niche strategies exist at one point or another along the Endgame life-cycle curve. Each industry sector has its own tempo and culture. Very often the unique characteristics of the industry sector are defined by the strengths and weaknesses of the sector leaders and global consolidators. Theoretically, all Endgame niche strategy opportunities are created by the strengths and weaknesses of the sector leader. If Adam Smith's invisible hand were all-powerful and all-knowing, there wouldn't be little pockets of unassailable competitive position. Every customer would have his or her needs met by a company that could produce the product or service for market value. Well, that obviously doesn't happen all the time.

But what does happen all the time is that niche fighters struggle and push against the sector leader and global consolidator until they lose, sell out, or simply don't care any more. Sometimes a sector has been redefined in such a way that the former sector leader is no longer relevant. In the early phases of the Endgame life-cycle curve, specialization and agility are important elements of a successful Endgame niche. In later phases, agility and freedom define the game-changing nature of successful Endgame niches.

Let's go back to the Value Building Growth database, which contains financial data on 32,000 public and 630,000 private companies across all industries around the world during a 15-year period. A.T. Kearney worked through these data to produce the Value Building Growth matrix and the Merger Endgame life-cycle curve, empirically proving—and disproving—many of the business strategy theorems of the past 20 years. In our Value Building Growth analysis, we track industry-sector players' sales growth and market capitalization growth and compare them to those of other companies in the same industry sector. In the Merger Endgame Theory analysis, we track the consolidation of industry sectors over time. First let's take a look at the results of the Value Building Growth matrix (see Figure 7-1).

The Value Building Growth matrix plots each company's performance. In the upper right quadrant are companies that grow faster than their competition and are also more highly valued by the market (in terms of market capitalization). We call these companies *value growers*, and usually only about 20 percent of compa-

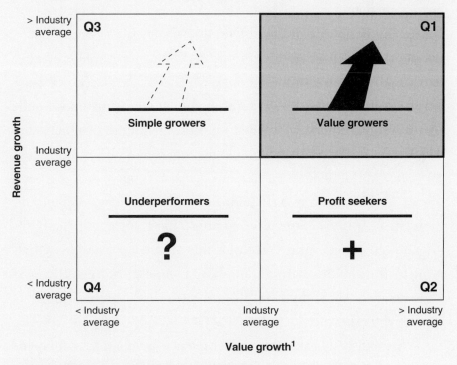

¹Measured as adjusted market capitalization growth = market capitalization growth adjusted for change in equity.
Sources: Value Building Growth database; A.T. Kearney analysis

Figure 7-1. Value Building Growth matrix

nies are in this quadrant in any given year. In the lower right quadrant are companies that we call *profit seekers*—these grow slower than the competition, but the market values them more highly. About 19 percent of companies fall into this category. Companies in the upper left quadrant—known as *simple growers*—grow more rapidly than the competition but also get dinged by the market. Only 14 percent of companies are represented here, because decreased market capitalization quickly limits a company's options for simple growth. Finally, the *underperformers* in the lower left quadrant—characterized by slow growth and below-average market capitalization—comprise about 47 percent of all companies in any given year.

Companies may move to different quadrants from year to year—ideally staying most of the time in the upper right quadrant, but periodically dashing to the left for a revenue growth spike or down for an organizational or structural shake-up to improve profitability. As you can imagine, it must be a pretty unique company that can stay in the upper right, value growing quadrant for more than 10 years. And indeed, less than one-tenth of 1 percent of the companies we studied were able to do so. In the upper right quadrant, there are only 600 companies that are stable Endgame niche fighters and have beaten the average sales and market capitalization growth of 665,730 of their toughest competitors over the past 15 years (see Appendix C for the complete list of stable Endgame niche fighters).

What can be learned from these clear winners in this competitive rumble? Following is a synopsis of each of the nine Endgame niches, with some examples. In Chapter 10 we'll flesh these out with in-depth case studies.

1. REGIONAL NICHES

It makes sense that regional niches are among the first to appear when new industry sectors are created. It also follows that regional niches are among the first to lose their power, as companies progressively exhaust all the regional market potential. As a matter of fact, in the Opening Phase and at the start of the Scale Phase, most of the players can be characterized as regional—because of either economic or regulatory issues. The economics of logistics keeps breweries regional relatively longer than insurance companies; the xenophobia and worry of the regulators keep banks regional longer than breweries.

The German beer market is a textbook example of a market that, for a long time, was shaped by regional customer preferences that originated from regulation. In 1516, the purity order imposed by Duke Wilhelm IV of Bavaria stipulated that beer could be produced only from yeast, hops, and water. This purity order, which still applies in Germany, also means that the German brewing industry is, with few exceptions, primarily restricted to the German market. This has resulted in an extremely large (93 percent) regional beer market.

With increasing deregulation of the foodstuffs market in Europe, it became possible to import into Germany foreign beer that was not brewed according to the specifications of the German purity order. To the great surprise of the German brewers, this was thoroughly successful. The German consumers were by no means as loyal to the unique flavor of German-brewed beer as the German brewers had assumed. In 2001, when the Dutch brewery Heineken bought a stake in the Schörghuber Group and Interbrew acquired Beck &

Co., even the unassailable German beer market had begun to crack. The objective of the global leaders was both to market their own product and to have a part of Europe's largest beer market.

Mineral water is another sector that has surprised many of the critics. Historically, most mineral water was sold around the local church towers in Europe, and logistical costs prevented water from being transported much more than 30 miles. This doesn't even begin to include the provincial "branding" element associated with close-to-home water. During the 1980s, the logistical constraints on distributing water started to decline. This period also saw the spectacularly aggressive marketing campaigns of what would become global brands—Evian, Pellegrino, and Gerolsteiner Sprudel.

Regional niches often exist because regulatory authorities believe that providers of products and services such as telecommunications, postal services, railways, airlines, energy utilities, banking, and insurance should be locally operated and controlled— to limit the power of outsiders in a national economy. The stated goal may be superior service for the consumers of these services, but the result is almost always protectionism unrelated to economics (and resulting inefficiency) for the providers of these services. When regulations are loosened and consumers are allowed to choose any company they want for these types of products and services, these regional niche strategies quickly crumble.

For example, until a few years ago, German regulators imposed rules that "protected" German consumers by assuring them certain technical specifications for their telephones. Despite the regulators' stated intentions, this meant that the telephones available in Germany were perhaps seven years behind the times and twice as expensive as those available elsewhere. Part of the reason for this is cultural, since regulations shape consumers' thoughts and feelings as well as producers' capabilities and constraints. Needless to say, however, this kind of noneconomic intervention is deemed less and less appropriate in the face of consumer demand.

There *are* important regional differences, though, and producers have to figure out how to deal with them. In the coffee market, despite almost total deregulation, the astonishing discovery was made that there are indeed different national coffee tastes. These are based on the characteristics and specific flavor that the coffee roasters that initially established each market have conditioned consumers to prefer. Europeans just shake their heads at the multibillion-dollar market for the watery brown liquid known as coffee in the United States. In Chile, the domestic market for red wine favored a distinctly oxidized finish—reportedly because that is what the Chileans had come to expect from high-priced European imported wines after they had spent months on the high seas. Local producers worked hard to achieve this corked flavor until well into the 1980s, when the growing export market started to demand the rich, fruity varietals that we associate with Chilean wines today. This kind of regional preference is hard to change, and is certainly more powerful than any regulation. The same also applies to the beer market, in which a number of specific types of beer—pilsner, Kölsch, Hefeweizen, export, import, malt, lager, ale, bock, black, shandies, nonalcoholic, light, bitter, pale, half, you name it—are being perpetuated into the future, with substantial, if not entirely understandable, consumer loyalty in each case.

The poster child for the regional niche continues to be the washing machine. Europeans favor a front-loading machine (in a stackable configuration, probably because of space restrictions), whereas Americans prefer the top-loading, side-by-side model. This poses a strategic question: Would the front-loading washing machine ever sell in the United States? Should companies even try? The growing Chinese electronics industry must decide which market to concentrate on; that is, it must decide which washing machine market and which product specification will be dominant in the future. It may decide to pursue both markets, which makes a lot of sense. Ford Motor Company didn't decide to make right-hand-drive cars for the Japanese market until the 1970s (even though it had tried to enter the Japanese market for decades before that). Sometimes producers think they can change consumer preferences. This is why regional niches often ultimately fail.

It should come as no surprise that regional niche strategies lose their effectiveness when global consolidators enter the Scale Phase and start buying up volume, regardless of strategic relevance. However, this doesn't always turn out successfully for the global consolidator. Wal-Mart's unhappy ventures into Germany and South Korea—where in each case it couldn't make the simple scale argument work and had to back out of the market—present perfect examples of "you win some, you lose some" in the Scale Phase. But Wal-Mart doesn't seem to be doing poorly lately. Regional niche strategies stopped working in Germany and South Korea a few years ago, but those markets still presented enough regional differences to trip up even this best of global consolidators.

Consider the mineral water market, discussed earlier, which is increasingly dominated by global brands and global consolidators Nestlé and Danone. Consider also the global beer market, which is similarly and very rapidly on its way to the Balance Phase with

Inbev, SABMiller, and Heineken blocking out their Endgame. Even the automobile industry is increasingly dominated by a few global brands—whether you know it or not. That's why Fords are beginning to look like Jaguars (while, happily, Jaguars are beginning to drive like Fords).

From the middle of the Scale Phase onward, regional niche fighters will be massively jeopardized as soon as the emerging sector leaders extend their expansion strategies to all regions.

Sometimes we are lulled into thinking that globalization is going on "behind the curtain," without making fundamental changes to our culture and consumer needs. But no one can deny that IKEA—whether in Chicago, Beijing, or Paris—has identified and serves a cross-cultural, needs-based market segment that is truly global. Starbucks does it, too, with a little more cultural distinction.

Subtle distinctions still remain—in Europe, Asia, the Middle East, and the Americas. Wal-Mart had a famous flop with its strait-laced refusal to take postdated checks in Brazil—a definite non-starter in a high-inflation consumer market. Reportedly, one of the reasons that Wal-Mart couldn't make a go of it in South Korea is that Korean shoppers actually like going from one place to the next, and didn't give Wal-Mart's one-stop-shop strategy the basket size needed to support this strategy. Also, regional authorities will sometimes impose seemingly strange requirements for things like opening and closing times, sale dates, and hiring practices. And then, of course, there are the exigencies of "nonstandard requirements" from local authorities. One top executive once told us, "I have two questions wherever I go: 'Can I open my business without bribing somebody, and can I keep my business open without bribing somebody once a year?' If the answer isn't, 'Yes, yes,' then I'm out of there. Life is too short, and the opportunity elsewhere is too great." Some regulations are even more subtle, or can change depending on how successful a company is.

Economic improvements in logistics in the past few decades have helped the process of eliminating the barriers to entry into regional bastions (along with easier transfer of funds and people). Thirty years ago, pundits would say, "Everything is global except for gravel pits, barbershops, and brothels." In the intervening years, the average service area for a concrete provider has grown from about a 30-mile radius to one of almost 300 miles, with global players taking bigger shares every day. Global players in the salon business are steadily aggregating hair-care delivery, along with professional product suppliers such as L'Oréal. As for the third sector, A.T. Kearney is leaving that analysis to others.

Regional and local tastes still drive demand, of course. This demand may wane with the influence of global communications, or it may grow, leading to bewildering developments; the Finns, for example, insist that they really like salty licorice chewing gum. We'll let companies decide for themselves how sensitive their product or service is to the enervating forces of global competition and consolidation.

2. TARGET-GROUP NICHES

The natural development of a successful regional niche is the target-group niche. In this type of niche, the target group extends beyond a single region. Regional niches grow into target-group niches when a company successfully expands to an adjoining or far-flung region and provides a product substantially similar to the one it originally offered in its home region. It may be Erdinger for German beer lovers in Georgia or a Harley Owners Group (H.O.G.) in Hamburg. Ideally, the target group must be served with a partially altered value chain, so that the major scale suppliers are not interested or are less competent than the niche fighter at achieving certain segment-specific scale effects. The transformation of Harley-Davidson during the 1990s is almost a textbook case of a successful target-group niche—moving from a middling manufacturer of motorcycles to a global purveyor of adventure lifestyles that captured the imaginations (and purchasing power) of customers with above-average educations and incomes.

Many target-group characteristics can be differentiating, including age, income level, gender, and occupation. However, occupation, lifestyle, and cultural orientation more often define target groups. Smart niche fighters must continue to refine their target group based on multiregional needs if they are to seamlessly migrate to more stable Endgame niches such as product and branding/ lifestyle niches.

A stronger orientation toward target groups is usually found in the middle of the Endgame Scale Phase, in which the successful niche fighters have exhausted the market potential of their initial region and are able to penetrate the adjoining regions. Fast-moving consumer goods, consumer durables, and most services are examples of industries in which target groups can be found and for which the potential for success is high.

The German market—with many homegrown players in many sectors—is a perfect laboratory for examining what happens when the protection that regional niche players once enjoyed is eliminated. Let's look at three sectors: banking, hotels, and automotive.

The increasing deregulation of the banking sector left the German banking market extremely fragmented, and most of the participants were regional niche players at best. In the 1990s, the Swiss, U.K., and U.S. commercial banks all expanded their own regional niches into target-group niches in Germany with target-group-oriented offers. For example, institutions such as UBS, Credit Suisse, Julius Baer, Vontobel, HSBC, Barclays, Lloyds TSB, and Abbey developed refined individual product ranges for wealthy private clients, penetrated the German market, and lured these clients away from the German top dogs. The German banks now no longer dominate this target group and are continuing to lose substantial amounts of assets, exposing them even further to the pressure of the global consolidators. Meanwhile, Citibank has been able to compete successfully against the regional savings banks, popular banks, and private banks with its private client business and continued business with the Post Office Bank.

The German savings bank sector currently serves approximately 51 percent of private banking clients, followed by the state banks, which serve 23 percent of this market. The question is: Will these banks be able to defend their regional niches given the increasing transparency of the market? While DekaBank was the market leader in 2006, with a market share of 20 percent, for five years running this investment savings bank has been losing market share.

The German banking sector is still years away from having a target-group orientation. This was demonstrated not long ago by market leader Deutsche Bank, which was uncertain as to whether it should serve private clients at all with its Bank 24 offering or sell Bank 24. This also applied to small-business clients. After an "exit campaign" at the start of 2000, which classified many clients with good credit ratings but without large cash assets as "less valuable," former Bank 24 clients are again being courted by Deutsche Bank. This inconsistent behavior has certainly not helped the stability of the client base.

In the United States, regional niche player Continental Bank made the same mistake in the mid-1990s, when it decided to focus on business accounts instead of on its established personal account business; neither business fared very well as a result. Ten years and six corporate generations later, Continental is now part of JPMorgan Chase, which has no problem serving both market segments. Continental couldn't move from a regional niche to a target-group niche, and was gobbled up during the Scale Phase.

Meanwhile, the German banking market is becoming increasingly consolidated. This is happening not only through takeovers, but also through the acquisition of target client groups by target-group niche fighters coming in from Switzerland, Scandinavia, the United Kingdom, the United States, and Holland that simply offer better, more tailored services. These target-group niche fighters recognize that if they don't act first outside their home region, they will remain regional niche players, susceptible to the global consolidators in the Endgame Scale Phase.

The hotel industry also had a regional focus. However, in the past 10 years, it has been increasingly dominated by multiregional target-group niche fighters with clearly defined product offerings and specific customer demographics. As a result, most German hoteliers have been taken out by foreign companies. The French Accor group was particularly successful in this sector with the Novotel, Mercure, and Ibis hotels. These hotels served the low-priced segment with a standardized product, offered at a standardized price nationwide, and were successful as a result. The similarly structured Dorint group, which initially focused on tax-saving properties, was taken over by the Accor group in 2003.

Five-star hotels in Germany are almost completely owned by foreign companies. Even the traditional German group Kempinski was sold in 1992 by the investor Dieter Bock to the Thai group Dusit Thani. Thus, Germany's hold on the regional hotel business has largely disintegrated. Many of the remaining German hotels in the five-star category are presumably nonprofit hobby investments of well-disposed entrepreneurs, with the Steigenberger Hotel Group perhaps being the only exception.

In the automobile industry, well-known brands such as Mercedes-Benz, Rolls-Royce, and Bentley have remained in the luxury market segments. Only Daimler-Benz managed to extend its product range to less affluent target groups—but it hit the curb with Smart and unwound the Chrysler deal after nine years, and now it's back to Daimler AG. The U.K. brands Rolls-Royce and Bentley, as well as Hispano-Suiza and Bugatti, could not extend beyond the luxury class segment because they were not able to leave their niche and build up larger scale effects.

Target-group strategies can therefore be considered a natural extension of regional niche strategies. Target-group strategies are usually successful if they are executed in different value chains. These chains must target segment-specific needs, which the niche supplier can then exploit to achieve scale advantages. Accordingly, these niches should be extended if the scale effects achieved through penetration in other regions make further scale effects possible. If, and only if, this is possible are target-group niches defendable long-term strategies.

As the global consolidators aggregate the overall market in the Endgame Scale Phase, regional niche players must decide whether to exploit their unique client base and value chain or maximize their sales value. In the first case, they have a chance to become a multiregional target-group niche fighter. In the second case, they get gobbled up.

3. PRODUCT NICHES

The product niche fighter concentrates on a subsidiary market that is clearly demarcated by a product. This product serves the relevant target group with a correspondingly dedicated value chain, individualized know-how, and specific commercial processes.

The essential factors for the success of such a strategy, which has been exemplified by the exceptional auto manufacturer Porsche, are that the value chain is so differentiated and the segment costs so structured that only the specialist niche supplier can achieve even approximate scale effects in the product segment. Even with their general scale effects, global consolidators cannot outbid the economies offered by successful product niche fighters.

Target-group niches and product niches come into play at about the same stage of the Endgame curve, and also evaporate at about the same time. The automotive industry demonstrates the factors that lead up to a product niche's demise. In this example, almost all suppliers started with a product focus. Throughout the course of industrial consolidation, these suppliers expanded to cover all product segments of the automobile market and aimed to match or even surpass the segment-specific cost advantages of the niche suppliers through their overall scale effects. How did this happen, and how did the global consolidators largely eliminate the product niche as a stable strategy in the automotive industry?

Toyota's rise is a classic example of expansion in all segments. Toyota's initial successes were achieved with mass automobile production and shrewd marketing to the lower middle class. Toyota then increasingly extended into the middle-class market with high-volume, high-quality models and favorable price-performance ratios. With the creation of Lexus as a subbrand in 1989, Toyota then directly confronted the upper-class market in Asia and North America and definitively left its original niche.

Many other major suppliers have evolved similarly. The best example is the auto manufacturers' expansion into the sports car and people-carrier segments. Both were initially dominated by pure product specialists and have now become part of the domain of the major brand manufacturers.

There are many examples of product niche players whose time has come and gone—not only Rolls-Royce and Bentley, but also Ferrari, Lamborghini, and Bugatti. All were initially successful with strong product niche positions, but were largely driven out of the market by expanding mass producers. The Ferrari group now belongs to the Fiat group, which is now under massive attack from the following competitors that are no longer niche suppliers:

- *Renault.* For a long time this car had the image of a French family car; its image now has a wider range.
- *Mercedes-Benz.* This brand also offers a broad product range across all product segments.
- *Toyota.* After large investments, particularly in technology and high-performance hybrids, this brand continues to improve.

It will be interesting to see whether smaller producers such as Daewoo can sustain a product niche, and how the emerging Chinese producers will balance their ready-made regional niche with a forward-thinking product niche strategy. In the course of the automobile Endgame, their survival as independent units or their departure from the market is surely only a question of time.

However, not all product niches are eclipsed by the global consolidators; two very successful examples can be found in BMW and Porsche. Through their product characteristics, these companies have been able to enjoy an "in-house evolution," distinct from the general market trend, for many years.

In 1975, BMW began to produce high-speed sedans for middle-class customers and was differentiated in this segment from then-market leaders Opel, Ford, and Daimler by higher speed capability and sportiness. This focus on a narrow segment was extended to the upper and lower market segments. Upper-class and upper-middle-class cars with very clear product characteristics—quick and sporty—then appeared on the market. This strategy has been so successful throughout the years that now, even in the German automobile market, BMW has a higher market share than its former major competitor, Daimler.

Daimler missed its chance in 1958, when it refused to purchase the completely reorganized Bayerische Motoren Werke. At this time, BMW was building the small car Isetta, which was not positioned very well in terms of brand, strategic consistency, or market success. Today, the tables are turned. Daimler is being forced by BMW's huge market success to restrict its focus to supplying fast and sporty limousines. BMW's success is so huge that in the United States—the largest automobile market in the world—it is now a more recognized brand than the legendary Daimler. It can be argued that BMW is becoming an effective branding niche fighter (which will be discussed next), combining unique product characteristics with target customer segmentation, and becoming a more stable niche fighter in the long term.

Similar developments can be observed in the pharmaceutical industry. In the past, vitamin products or special therapeutic applications were supplied by independent companies. These companies have now been taken over by the huge pharmaceutical groups such as Pfizer, GlaxoSmithKline, AstraZeneca, Novartis, and sanofi-aventis. Many of the smaller biotechnology companies are now being consolidated and, in the near or distant future, will belong to the major pharmaceutical companies as the value of their innovations is realized. The scale effects of the pharmaceutical companies are so superior, especially in market-facing processes, that future mergers appear unavoidable.

The foodstuffs sector is similarly vulnerable. Whether product niche strategies will enjoy long-term success in this sector remains to be seen. Take the example of global consolidator Nestlé. Consolidation started with the chocolate industry, then the mineral water market, and now the ice cream market is being attacked (until recently, this market was still in the hands of small regional suppliers). Will the product segments that are currently independent—such as the jams market, which is currently dominated by regionally focused suppliers—survive the consolidation?

Major companies such as Procter & Gamble and Gillette, which recently merged, were both clear market leaders in specific and different product segments. However, both companies had numerous value-chain overlaps in supplying the equally consolidated retail industry. Keeping this in mind, the days that small regional players will remain independent are numbered.

Sometimes an aggressive product niche fighter can push the market leader right up to the edge. An example of an extremely successful product niche fighter is Alcan, which overtook Alcoa as the aluminum sector's market leader. At a 2002 business conference in Toronto on the subject of the Merger Endgame, an Alcan representative remarked that the company had deliberately targeted the weaknesses of Alcoa, and that it was only a matter of a few years before it would overtake the market leader. The man was obviously right. If the growth positions of 2002 are compared to the growth positions of 2005, it is apparent that Alcan was on the best possible route to achieving its goal. Alcan's takeover of the French aluminum manufacturer Pechiney was just one example of a step in the right direction. In this case, the counter niche strategy ran its course. Alcan and Alcoa were unable to dominate each other, and Alcan was sold to Rio Tinto for a very good price in 2007.

One of the most successful product niches is CNN, which was developed in 1980 by Ted Turner. CNN entered the broadcasting market with a very narrow product focus. It positioned itself against the established television channels in the United States and provided global coverage in the news segment. Established competitors such as NBC, ABC, and CBS sat and watched the developments in this rapidly growing segment as CNN captured viewers with legendary success during the first Gulf War. CNN then continued to enjoy success, even though the established broadcasters also entered this market. CNN's advantages, however, which were based on its control of the distribution channels, eventually reduced the stability of its product niche strategy. CNN is now part of the larger media group Time Warner. The broadcaster's national companies are struggling as a result of the counteractions of the established players.

The establishment of overnight express package delivery by United Parcel Service and Federal Express equally trumped the formerly powerful logistics suppliers. Almost all of them—including Kühne + Nagel and Danzas—attempted to imitate this market as followers, but they were not able to do so. The specialist suppliers were able to build their advantages of scale early on for this relatively narrow product/service range on the basis of different commercial processes, very different customer-facing approaches designed for the nonspecialist customer, and, to some extent, different value structures.

Now the express couriers are beginning to compete with the formerly established logistics groups for larger-scale shipping and forwarding. Once again, this shows that niche strategies are successful only if they are rapidly and consistently implemented, and implemented more rapidly and more consistently than the strategies of potential imitators.

4. BRANDING/LIFESTYLE NICHES

When a product niche fighter can match its unique product and tailored value chain with the needs of a target customer segment and communicate its benefits through a brand, it can unleash one of the strongest and most stable niche strategies—the branding niche. Branding niche fighters can pursue this strategy through the Endgame Scale Phase and well into the Focus Phase.

A convincing, well-managed brand does not fall from the sky. It is created by linking high quality and service with a brand name and by building credibility with the customer in a progressive, continuous way. The brand must achieve lots of recognition, and customers must be moved over time before they become loyal purchasers. Also required is consistent service and quality that, ideally, differentiate the company from the competition. The longer such loyalty continues and is not abused by the supplier, the more the brand achieves emotional characteristics. This ensures that customers' purchasing decisions are not purely rational.

To ensure the service promised in the brand, its structure should be appropriately adjusted to provide a unique combination of market segments and value-creation structures that makes the branding niche increasingly difficult for the global consolidators to penetrate. An established branding niche becomes more and more difficult to penetrate from outside. The automobile industry illustrates this. Initially, the automobile industry supplied necessary and reliable technical services. However, with the passage of time, the purchase or operation of an automobile came to depend increasingly on emotional factors. It is not a stretch to say that personal identity is reflected in specific automobiles.

Particularly in Germany, there are clear differences in marketing among automakers BMW, Daimler, Porsche, Audi, Volkswagen, Opel, and Ford. They all have loyal target customer groups. Accordingly, the automobile market in Germany is defined by clear client loyalties, which remain stable as long as the quality initiatives that stand behind a brand remain consistent. Of course, this does not always happen, as seen with the Mercedes-Benz brand, which for several years in succession has been clearly beaten in the quality ratings by the Japanese suppliers, Audi, and BMW. S-Class sales were in decline as a result, and Mercedes began recording losses for the first time in many decades (although sales have recently recovered). The group's operating profit was affected in 2004. Despite these effects, it is still quite difficult to get into the German automobile market because the customer is so attached to the established names.

In markets such as the United States, where emotional attachment to the established European brands is not as great, Japanese brands such as Lexus and Infinity, for example, are capturing a substantially higher market share than in the German upper-class category. In the United States, price-performance ratio is what counts.

The brand Porsche, with products "which in fact nobody needs" (as the head of Porsche, Wendelin Wiedeking, mused), has become, through the development and exploitation of well-established and very stable customer loyalty, the most profitable automobile company in the world. Recently, Porsche was even able to take cross-holdings in the largest automobile producer in Europe, Volkswagen. This amount of success is thanks to Porsche's brand, for which the founders of the company are responsible. Meanwhile, the highly competent Wiedeking, Porsche's chief executive, is responsible for the brand's renewed vigor. Indeed, the strength of Porsche's brand is so great that it is the dream of every young German man to drive a Porsche at least at one time in his life. A recent television spot shows a nine-year-old boy going into a Porsche dealer and asking technical questions about the car. The boy takes a business card from the salesman and then says he will be back in 20 years. This is precisely a reflection of this brand identity.

It remains to be seen how long Porsche will be able to sustain its brand, which was initially based on a unique speed advantage, because speed has become a me-too competence in this market.

Speed is now equally offered by BMW, Audi, Toyota, Renault, Mercedes-Benz, and other emotionally charged brands such as Ferrari, Maserati, Lamborghini, and Lotus. But it is the same all over the world; brands that were once strong in a particular region can expand their reach.

A unique branding niche has been created by Montblanc. This brand originally appeared as a manufacturer of high-quality fountain pens, and until the mid-1980s, it was successful to a limited extent in the higher end of the market. In Germany, Montblanc was known only as a fountain pen brand. In 1996, the company was bought by the Richemont group in South Africa and thereafter was built into a world-renowned icon. The brand was initially marketed intensely to the upper segment of the writing-goods market, and then extended to limited editions of "writing jewelry" that were sold for completely irrational prices. These editions have now become a side market and are acquired at collector's prices. In the writing-goods sector, the new branding strategy has been so successful that the other manufacturers of high-quality writing goods (Waterman, Pelikan, Rotring, Lamy, Parker, and Schaeffer) have been driven out or, in some cases, propelled irreversibly into lower-price segments.

To summarize Montblanc's history, the U.K. tobacco and lifestyle brand Dunhill acquired a majority holding in the company in the 1970s. After Dunhill Holdings had increased its share in Montblanc from 66 to 91 percent, it was acquired by Rothmans International. Rothmans, in turn, was taken over by Philip Morris, from which Montblanc was bought little by little by the Richemont group, which finally acquired the entire brand in 1993. Contrary to all expectations, the brand Montblanc now represents far more than writing equipment and thus, after a "rebranding," has become a completely unique market of its own. In essence, Montblanc has almost no competition, as it has created its own lifestyle market with extraordinary utility objects for successful and ambitious people. This was possible because of the strength of its outstanding brand, which now exists almost independently of the product.

Montblanc's strategy has been so successful that it currently produces 130,000 watches annually. It is predicted that in the year 2010, writing goods will represent only 50 percent of all of Montblanc's sales. The next target group envisaged is women, as women make up 60 percent of boutique clients. Women, who purchase Montblanc products for their husbands but also for themselves, will likely be approached directly with appropriate products that fit their own requirements.

Automobile brands Rolls-Royce and Bentley enjoy similar brand identities. At the time they were acquired by BMW and Volkswagen, respectively, these companies were not capable of delivering the quality that their established brands claimed. Image and reality were miles apart. However, the new owners, interested in their own brand extension, have reinstated the high quality and reliability of these brands; this will give these well-known brands their former resonance.

Branding niche strategies are vulnerable unless the branding niche fighter can craft a value chain that is distinct, differentiated, and immune to attack. Naya Water created a vibrant, differentiated, sporty brand of bottled water and had significant success until Coca-Cola, which had been distributing Naya through its network, decided to introduce a purified tap water product in its own product line. Overnight, Naya lost its advantaged—but undifferentiated—value chain, and even its powerful brand could not save it. Naya is now a Danone brand.

Particularly in consumer brands, the relative weight and power of the manufacturer's brand versus the retailer's in-house brand adds another dimension to the branding niche strategy. Stable branding niche fighters such as Victoria's Secret, Coach, and Tiffany are giving their corresponding manufacturer brands (Jockey, Fruit of the Loom, and Hanes, for example) a real run for their money.

On the subject of branding niches, we might make the following conclusion: If you can build a brand's personality with a clear product promise over a certain period of time and give it an emotional charge, then you can establish a branding niche that is able to be defended against the global consolidators, especially in the luxury or technology-intensive segments.

5. Speed/Lightning-Consolidation Niches

In a speed niche, the niche fighter attempts to achieve the scale effects of the market leaders or overtake them. It does this either by occupying speed segments or through rapid consolidation. With Internet technology, speed niches appear frequently. While market caps can still be impressive (such as Facebook's recent peg at $15 billion), the niche fighter's long-term success depends on how well the Internet-based technology is integrated into the consumers' cash flow and how impervious it is to attack from the next big thing.

Amazon.com was an early speed niche fighter, and it might have stumbled if it hadn't gotten its physical distribution capabilities in order. The industry-supported Internet exchanges of the early 2000s serve as examples: Covisint, WorldWide Retail Exchange, Transora, and GlobalNetXchange (GNX) have undergone their own "speed consolidation" as positioning in the marketplace became less and less differentiated.

Many Chinese companies are executing speed niche strategies as the global market rushes to serve the emerging Chinese middle class. With the help of the Chinese government, otherwise subscale competitors are being transformed into multibillion-dollar overnight competitors. Consider the retailer Bailian. While this strategy can stave off the global consolidators temporarily, longer-term success depends on the ability of these new, larger speed niche players to achieve the economies of scale that will allow them to compete effectively against such global consolidators as Wal-Mart, Carrefour, and Metro. India's Reliance is investing more than $6 billion in India's organized retail industry *in anticipation* of the global consolidators entering the Indian market in earnest. Aditya Birla is following the same approach. In this way, Reliance and Aditya Birla are strengthening their bulwarks against global consolidation.

In the retail industry, we have seen the "category killers"— those stores that offer a category-specific shopping experience with comprehensive coverage—attempt to apply a speed niche strategy. However, their success depends on the consumer's interest level in shopping at an establishment with this kind of format. Home Depot's rapid consolidation of the home repair/do-it-yourself sector found favor in the United States, as did B&Q in the United Kingdom, attracting consumers who were fed up with having to go to three or four different stores for the materials needed for a single project. Speed niche aggregation has also worked as a stable niche strategy in office supplies, pet supplies, and, of course, books and toys.

In cosmetics, on the other hand, this strategy hasn't fared as well, with consumers preferring to segment their purchases among drugstores, department stores, and specialty boutiques. For example, beauty.com, which was touted years ago as being "poised to take over the online beauty market," is now part of online retail aggregator drugstore.com. Brick-and-mortar competitors such as Cosmetics Plus went bankrupt. In the end, most category killers did the global consolidators a favor by taking out the mom-and-pop outlets before quietly being taken out themselves.

Further speed-niche success stories are to be found among the low-cost aviation carriers. Companies such as Ryanair, easyJet, Hapag-Lloyd Express, and Air Berlin (which came from the charter business, similar to Southwest Airlines in North America) offered a clearly defined, standardized offer with low prices and acceptable service. They were able to displace the established high-priced carriers. In Europe, these low-cost carriers currently have a market share of 25 percent. This speed-niche attack forced the established leaders, including Lufthansa, to respond. Lufthansa developed its subsidiary Germanwings to counter these offers. Lufthansa's high level of service, with all its associated comforts, is not available to Germanwings flyers, and this is emphatically made clear to them in all communications. Aer Lingus, on the other hand, makes less of such distinctions, but you can still fly round trip from Heathrow to Dublin for £6 sterling.

A subset of the speed niche is *lightning consolidation*, in which a dramatic series of acquisitions creates short-term, successful integration and new scale effects. Through lightning consolidation of the Russian steelworks that formerly existed in the Eastern Bloc, the Indian steel entrepreneur Mittal acquired a world market leadership position. With the acquisition of Arcelor, Mittal reached a stable position against all newcomers. And with the delisting of ABN AMRO after its acquisition by a consortium led by Royal Bank of Scotland, ArcelorMittal joined the NYSE Stoxx 50. It has practically doubled its value in a 12-month period. Not bad for a three-year-old! The only competitors that ArcelorMittal has to fear will be Baosteel and China Steel, which are growing at similarly high speeds and are also highly profitable.

However, not all speed niches are successful. The e-business bubble at the end of the 1990s and the highly specialized e-business consultants such as Razorfish, Sapient, and marchFIRST serve as highly publicized examples of failure. They attempted—for a short time with real success—to focus on e-business consulting and rapid growth as a way of overtaking the established market leaders such as McKinsey, Boston Consulting Group, A.T. Kearney, and Bain & Company. However, after the popping of the "bubble," they were forced to recognize that their speed had actually led to their failure.

The essential factor for the success of speed niches, in addition to focusing on speed, is the early creation of segment-specific advantages. These can be created either through a customer experience or through value-chain economies that cannot be countered by the established global consolidators. Speed will get companies where they want to go and allow them to fight against the global consolidators, but speed is only one ingredient for success. However, market leaders and global consolidators are sometimes arrogant and slow. What would have happened if Mercedes-Benz had taken the new competitor BMW seriously sooner and responded rapidly and flexibly with a new series of fast, medium-class sedans? In terms of financial capacity, know-how, and an apparently unassailable image, the brand Mercedes-Benz would have been the hands-down winner in such a struggle. However, Mercedes-Benz was self-satisfied at the time and not ready for a fight.

Thus, Lufthansa, although an established market leader in Europe, is being prudent and logical in its move to offer cheap flights through Germanwings. It remains to be seen whether the two contrasting cultures—the conservative, customer-oriented Lufthansa and the newer Germanwings, which offers no special comforts to customers—can be successfully combined under a single roof.

6. Innovation Niches

Innovation is certainly the broadest of all niche categories. Innovation not only relates to market segmentation and parts of the value chain, but can extend across the entire range of operational activities as well as market entry. Innovation therefore results not only in a breakthrough alteration, renewal, or improvement of a product range, but also in permanent changes and adjustments of all the value and marketing activities. A company that introduces an innovative customer-management process or effectively restructures direct-marketing strategies is just as innovative as a company that develops new product features or releases completely new products to the market every year.

Innovation niches are by definition more extensive and complex than other niches. At the same time, innovation niches always overlap with other forms of Endgame niche strategies. Innovation can relate to a product and therefore change a product niche. Innovation has a strong influence on a brand and can help establish a new branding niche. Everything that goes beyond purely building scale and deliberately introducing new elements into the market to increase value should be regarded as innovative and therefore should fit into this category.

There are numerous books on innovation, and we all imagine that innovation is the product of serendipity—like an apple falling from the tree. But companies that successfully assert themselves as innovation niche fighters often use what is called a "stretch tool-box." Figure 7-2 offers the steps that a company must take to

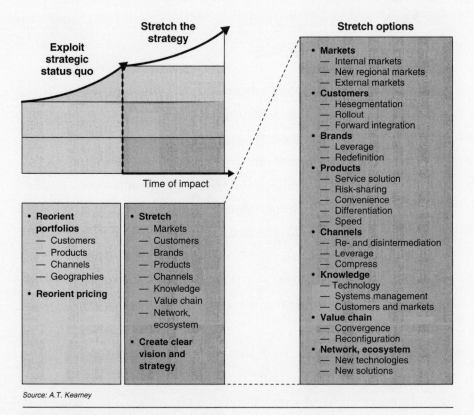

Source: A.T. Kearney

Figure 7-2. The stretch toolbox

improve its brand, product, and processes and align them with its customers' values.

Numerous other innovation approaches relate only to relatively superficial changes in a product. For example, the Blue Ocean Strategy devised by W. Chan Kim and Renée Mauborgne argues that tomorrow's leading companies will succeed not by battling competitors, but by creating "blue oceans" of uncontested market space for growth. This approach can only result in changes that are inadequately anchored in the value-creation structure and thus will not provide a company with a strategic defense. Only if innovations can be defended, either through patents or corresponding control of the value-creation structure, do they constitute a niche strategy, and provide security against the scale advantages of market leaders.

However, as we will demonstrate later, an Endgame innovation niche fighter has other advantages over large market leaders, which may not react to significant innovations in product or service offers quickly enough and therefore may lose market share. The main levers for innovation are products, customer (or client) services, and new technologies, which ideally increase advantages for the customer. Analyses have shown that the following 10 innovation strategies are particularly successful in building value that leads to growth:

1. *Solutions to problems.* Not only must the innovation address a real customer need, but the innovative solution must be communicated to and valued by the consumer as well. German luxury automobiles seem to provide more value than their customers perceive in the area of electronics. In conversations with many drivers, it became apparent that they could perceive the value of this innovation to only a limited

extent. Thus, are the Japanese automobiles better oriented toward communicating value in the long term with their top quality and simple operability?

2. *Service offers.* Since the deregulation of the German insurance market, the Anglo-Saxon insurance companies have triumphed over the established German top dogs. This was achieved not only through better pricing, but also by offering substantial innovations in service such as more flexible policies and payment options, additional information, and estate planning. The same is true in banking. How else can the market share of foreign banks such as UBS, Goldman Sachs, Credit Suisse, First Boston, and Morgan Stanley among high-net-worth clients and the complete stagnation of the German credit institutions be explained?

3. *Increased speed.* The entire logistics sector has changed with the introduction of the speed category, exemplified by Federal Express. The logistics-sector companies with the highest capital are now UPS, with a market capitalization of $74 billion, and Federal Express, with a market capitalization of $31 billion. All of this reflects the importance of speed and time flexibility.

4. *Convenience.* The initial offer of frozen meals by the German-based firm apetito in 1958 largely revolutionized the foodstuffs market in Germany. To everyone's surprise, many of the established food manufacturers, including Unilever and Nestlé, have hardly been able to counter this innovation. Apetito is now a stable niche fighter in Europe, with an emphasis on convenience and tailored partner solutions, rather than on mass-market offerings. This convenience

product was originally limited to a relatively narrow customer segment. However, apetito is defending its niche. Its products are now offered by many of the largest commercial chains, and, importantly, the company maintains higher-than-average profits.

5. *Microsegmentation.* In contrast to European markets, the U.S. market for consumer durables is largely dominated by target-group niche fighters. These include companies such as Brookstone, with sales of $490 million, Hammacher Schlemmer, with sales of $749 million, and commercial chains such as Sharper Image that aim at narrow customer segments. Tchibo in Germany has also modeled its success on microsegmentation, in many cases creating microsegments for its quickly changing specialty items. Its motto is "every week a new world."

6. *Results orientation.* Taking responsibility for outcomes rather than just touting selling points creates an innovative halo around any product or service, providing a value that customers will recognize and reward—either by paying higher prices or with brand loyalty. In management consulting, for example, taking responsibility for the results of a consulting engagement has opened up substantial new market possibilities, which have led from pure strategy to implementation, or at least implementation planning. This approach enables the client to achieve substantially more value than a mere strategy would. How would the sales of power stations be affected if, for example, Siemens or ABB were not just to sell power stations, but also to take over megawatts or the operation of the power stations over time? In this case, a stronger

results orientation of the supply would seem to make sense, since these companies have superior know-how in the technology and maintenance of power stations. The recent trend for most auto manufacturers to provide five-year, bumper-to-bumper warranty coverage reinforces the important effect of this type of innovation on brand value. It makes a huge difference when the manufacturer is willing to take on a customer's car maintenance, at least until the customer is done making the car payments!

7. *Risk sharing.* Sharing risks between supplier and customer in innovative ways is closely connected with results-oriented innovation. Innovation is achieved through rearranging the way total risk is divided among the various players in a transaction—as the previous auto-warranty example shows. Other industry sectors reflect completely different kinds of risk profiles. In Europe, for example, unnaturally low occupancy rates in commercial rental properties might be remediated if a more "liquid" approach to commercial property existed. Although the subprime loan debacle of 2007 could have been avoided, it does show that the identification and commercialization of risk creates not only valuable innovation, but also entirely new kinds of secondary or derivative risk.

8. *New markets.* Since the middle of the 1990s, the island of Majorca off the coast of Spain has evolved from a destination with mass-market appeal and cheap prices to a premium brand with increased profits. This has been accomplished through Majorca's entry into new tourism and travel markets. For example, Majorca has become a favored destination for golfers and conventioneers. With the construction of the

Congress Centre in Palma, and its new five-star hotels and excellent golf courses, Majorca has captured a substantial portion of both the golf and convention markets simply through a new market presentation. The attraction will continue to grow with the addition of art galleries and further infrastructure expansion. Similarly, the inconspicuous ski village of Davos in Switzerland comes alive each January when it hosts the global phenomenon of the World Economic Forum Annual Meeting. Jackson Hole, Aspen, and even Monaco are revving up their marketing efforts; in Monaco, Prince Albert is charting the development of his tiny principality for the next 650 years.

9. *Brand and customer stretch.* Beiersdorf, initially a manufacturer of basic skin-care products, achieved market recognition with everyday products such as NIVEA cream, which was initially billed as the indispensable hand cream for housewives and children. Over the past 10 years, the company has reinvented the NIVEA brand, achieving a well-thought-out and successful entry into the cosmetics market by expanding its line to face creams, hair care, deodorants, and cosmetics. This *stretch* move, which increased sales from $3.9 billion in 1994 to $6.5 billion in 2004, addressed target groups that the company had not previously reached, such as female clients who used more sophisticated products and men with skin- and hair-care regimens. The NIVEA brand is now on its way to becoming a leading global body-care brand, surpassing the existing market leaders Dove, Olay, and Neutrogena, which are offered by Procter & Gamble, Unilever, and Johnson & Johnson, respectively.

10. *Sales channels.* CeWe Color, the European market leader in photo services, can attribute its rise from the ranks of small suppliers to an early focus on mass sales channels. Today, it sells photo processing and related products through the major mass retailers, including Schlecker, Metro, Tengelmann, Drospa, and Rossmann—a move that opened up new mass markets and a scale that led to market leadership in Europe. Meanwhile, U.S. market leader Kodak wavered on how to address digital media in the 1980s and 1990s, allowing innovative Japanese and European companies an opening into its near-monopoly on photo processing.

The Internet distribution channel has totally changed transaction costs in distribution and thus created a host of niche markets. In his recent book, *The Long Tail: Why the Future of Business Is Selling Less of More*, Chris Anderson outlines how the Internet has essentially abolished the 80:20 rule, using examples from the digital world such as how movies, music, and information are distributed online via Amazon.com, eBay, and every online community where members share experiences and opinions.

There are many innovation strategies that can be used throughout all stages of value creation and market development. Before employing any of these strategies, however, it is essential to consider several factors. For example, to what extent will the new product or service be able to satisfy actual or latent customer requirements? How can the innovation niche fighter develop a secure moat around its market leadership? Innovations should also fly under the radar of the global consolidators, or be sufficiently off their development tracks, so that the innovation niche fighter has a window of opportunity to develop scale and market advantages.

7. COOPERATION NICHES

Another way niche companies can avoid being devoured by the scale leaders is by forming cooperative arrangements with other companies seeking a stable niche strategy. Cooperations can be formed by linking with other companies as a group or at parts of the value chain to jointly achieve scale effects that are comparable or even superior to those of the market leaders.

Even in industries that are precluded from merger Endgame consolidation by regulation or some other constraint, cooperation niche strategies can have a powerful impact. A good example is the Star Alliance, an airline partnership whose members include Lufthansa, Air Canada, Air New Zealand, All Nippon Airways, Asiana Airlines, Austrian Airlines, Spanair, Scandinavian Airlines, United, US Airways, Thai Airways International, Varig, and others. The alliance allows member airlines to share technology platforms and customer-service processes, while customers gain access to premium airport lounges and discounts and can earn and redeem frequent flyer miles. This alliance of equal, major competitors has resulted in a substantial competitive advantage. Subsequently, the cooperation niche model has been adopted by British Airways, American Airlines, Finnair, and others (the oneworld alliance) and by Air France, Delta, KLM, and others (the SkyTeam airline alliance).

Other companies that have achieved dramatic savings through cooperation niches are purchasing corporations such as Covisint, cc-hubwoo, and LSN. Still, these types of cooperations were initially not very successful. For example, when Ferdinand Piëch, former chairman of the board of Volkswagen, was asked why he did not want to participate in such cooperation niches, he responded, "I am not going to make my purchasing advantages available to my competitors." Wal-Mart notoriously goes it alone. The rest of the retail industry works together globally with innovative solutions from Agentrix, which is the merged product of the two big retail exchanges WorldWide Retail Exchange and GNX.*

The research sector has witnessed similar resistance from global consolidators, as questions are always raised concerning who can use what research results and to what extent. Still, there have been a handful of successful research cooperations. One example is the former research cooperation between Daimler-Benz and Mitsubishi, established in 1994 on the initiative of former chairman of the board Edward Reuter. This cooperation, which was launched with a great deal of publicity, started well and led to Daimler-Benz holding shares of Mitsubishi. However, the holding ended in 2004, when it became apparent that the financial obligations that Daimler took over from Mitsubishi were far greater than the group's capacities at the time.

Even collaboration that is temporary and will eventually be dissolved should be considered. In this regard, Ford Motor Company's recently announced cooperation with Daimler to buy Ballard Power Systems and develop automotive fuel cell technology makes a lot of sense. These two, though not likely to be Endgame winners because of their overall competitive positions in the Value Building Growth matrix, are seeking ways to continue their independence and survival. Such cooperation agreements are not usually envisioned as long-term alliances. A well-planned cooperation is a sensible model for achieving advantageous scale effects in the era of global con-

---

*Mike Moriarty and Bruce Klassen, *Power Play: The Beginning of the Endgame in Net Markets* (New York: John Wiley & Sons, 2001).

solidation. It should be maintained only as long as both partners perceive that they are drawing equally strong advantages from the cooperation, or at least as much as they need to stave off the amorous advances of the global consolidators.

Apart from the aviation companies, there are not very many major cooperations to point to. This can easily be explained by the fact that many industries are not yet in the Balance Phase of the Endgame curve and—unlike the air travel industry—are not the focus of noneconomic regulatory constraints. As a result, they are exposed to the intense competition among industrial partners in earlier phases. A long-term voluntary collaboration is not possible in a phase that is still highly competitive. However, there are certain sectors that can and should take advantage of industrywide cooperation, including energy generation and distribution, telephonic communication, outsourced IT, facilities management, and other shared services. This brings us to the next kind of stable niche strategy.

8. MARKET-SPLITTING NICHES

As industry sectors consolidate and move up the Merger Endgame curve, many players wonder if consolidation is inevitable, or if there are ways to ultimately fight off the global consolidators. We have discussed a number of strategies that permit Endgame niche fighters to achieve and retain stability. But by and large, these strategies operate within the sector that is being consolidated. Market splitting, or the creation of new markets by splitting partial markets into individual markets, is the most pronounced form of niche strategy.

If they are successful, market-splitting niche fighters can largely escape the attack of global consolidators and possibly achieve scale in a self-defining industry sector. Here the sector is redefined so that it operates as if it were in the Opening Phase of the Merger Endgame; one company comes up with a good market-splitting idea and attracts other entrants, thus reducing concentration within the sector. Then, as the players in the new sector sort out, they move into the Scale Phase, where efficiency and leverage become important, and so on and on. This allows another 25 years of strategic growth and development for a market splitter and represents the execution of a stable Endgame strategy.

In many respects, the stability of other Endgame niche strategies is dependent on scale and changing the definition of scale. For example, it is possible to defend a regional niche by segmentation and specialization to such an extent that the global consolidators decide that they cannot penetrate it, or at least they do not find penetrating it to be strategically interesting. In other words, the prospects of long-term stability are limited both by the effectiveness of the Endgame niche fighter's actions and by the responses of global competitors and other players. The question is, can a customer segment be isolated so that it is no longer vulnerable to the superior efficiency of the global consolidators?

Innovation niches provide stability for Endgame niche fighters as long as the innovation in question cannot be quickly reproduced by global consolidators in a more efficient manner. So, as long as innovation niche fighters are thriving on first-mover advantage, their survival depends on how quickly their competitors react. This was the fatal flaw of many of the Internet-based innovators of the 1990s. However, if innovation niches also manage to develop the innovation into product niches, with their own value-chain dynamics and their own target group, these new niches can achieve stability.

A branding niche fighter can definitely create its own stable markets based on the emotional aspects of its brand. Harley-Davidson is certainly not purely a motorcycle supplier any more than Porsche is purely a car manufacturer. Rolls-Royce's brand has value, even without a particularly competitive automobile behind it, as is also the case with Bentley—they both integrate the automotive technologies of other companies and deliver them in a valuable brand. Montblanc, Hermès, and Davidoff have all managed to detach their brands from their products' origins, replacing them with an independent lifestyle and a proprietary value chain.

Now let's turn our focus to splitting the value chain into individual product and service supply chains, which create their own new markets. Since the introduction of the corporate genome concept, the possibility of freely combining independent elements of value creation has become important to a company's strategic orientation. The authors of *Rebuilding the Corporate Genome: Unlocking the Real Value of Your Business* assert that by developing Web-based technology and the free flow of knowledge and intellectual property, the individual elements of the value chain, and the skills required to create and reconfigure them, will become freely "combinable."[†] This is much like the logistics revolution of the 1970s and the development of free-flowing global capital markets in the 1980s. As a result, the scale of transaction times and costs can be reduced, in theory, to zero.

[†]Johan C. Aurik, Gillis J. Jonk, and Robert E. Willen, *Rebuilding the Corporate Genome: Unlocking the Real Value of Your Business* (Hoboken, N.J.: John Wiley & Sons, 2002).

This fundamental shift in the underlying economics of corporate formation not only opens up the possibility of new market opportunities, but also could actually require them. This is very much like the changes in the global flow of capital, goods, and labor that required the epochal shifts in corporate structure and competitiveness that we have witnessed over the past 40 years. And once these new markets are created, with new entrants and players, the Merger Endgame Theory predicts the path they will pursue in the consolidation of these new markets (see Figure 7-3).

In the early 1900s, the automobile manufacturers, like all other producers at that time, were vertically integrated. They began at the outset with an extremely flat value chain. Ford Motor Company, for example, even owned the sheep that produced the wool for the head-

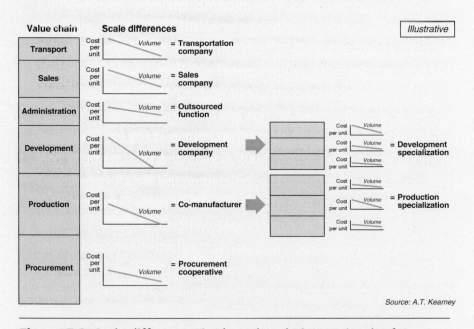

Figure 7-3. Scale differences in the value chain require the formation of new market segments

liners in its early models. Over the decades, a complex web of new industries was created, driven by consumer demand for vehicles and by increasing refinements in products and production technology that allowed individual elements of the value chain to become independent. Ultimately, independent market sectors for vehicle systems—brakes, engines, gears, seats—that would have been unthinkable in the industry's infancy were created. The ensuing collaboration of the suppliers and the automobile industry was always close, if not always friendly.

In the last decades of the twentieth century, whole functions were hived off in the form of procurement companies, development companies, and parts manufacturers. The resultant automotive original equipment manufacturers, or OEMs, as they are now known, focused on design, assembly, and marketing—functions in which they could apply their global scope and scale. In the 1990s, this process was largely complete, with even the majors, General Motors and Ford, splitting off their big in-house suppliers, Delphi and Visteon, to create huge supply conglomerates.

The Merger Endgame Theory would predict that this kind of forced market splitting would expose the resulting players to a potentially riotous free market. And, indeed, this was the case. The new entities underwent several years of significant restructuring and consolidation, with their competitive positions now depending less and less on their founders. Denso, the corresponding supplier to Toyota, was segregated during the post-World War II dismantling of the Japanese "war machine." These same trends take place in virtually every industry sector, from footwear to computer peripherals.

Speaking of the footwear industry, we have to wonder when the split-off will occur. When will the production facilities that have secured the volumes of adidas and parts of Puma and Nike realize that they have achieved sufficient scale effects and can rely on their collective know-how to offer their own brands in the global market? No one knows for sure. But certainly the experience of Danone, which started developing its products with Chinese partner Wahaha only to find the latter much more aggressive in serving the burgeoning Chinese market, stands as an example of how entrepreneurs can advance their businesses at the expense of global consolidators. So it is with market-splitting niche fighters and the companies from which they spring. Splitting the value chain and marketing its individual stages can result in stable, independent niches.

A spectacular example of this is Standard Application Programming (SAP). In 1972, SAP split off from the German IBM subsidiary and started to offer programming services as an independent product. Now, in its own market for standard operating software, SAP is in a race with Oracle for market leadership. In turn, Oracle, a database software company, is seeking to become a full-service supplier, and therefore a competitor to be taken seriously by SAP, through the acquisition of application software companies. The Merger Endgame created by the market-splitting niche fighter SAP in 1972 has run a predictable course in the past three decades, and is now late in its global consolidation phase.

Intel serves as another example. The company moved early and created its own market for chip production; it quickly achieved scale effects and competitive advantage. This, in turn, forced integrated manufacturers Siemens and Philips to split off their own chip-production functions. The result was relatively unsatisfactory, since today this market remains in the firm grasp of the Americans, with a market share of 81 percent.

Personal computers were also an original part of IBM's product portfolio at the beginning of the 1980s, but they were soon marketed only halfheartedly, even if "IBM-compatible" remained a key concept for a long time. The customer-facing processes, customer offers, and processes just weren't within IBM's sweet spot. Instead, first Compaq and then Dell took over the large-scale production and marketing of PCs; Dell enthusiastically brought this product to clients in its own market sector. Thus, it was no surprise when in 2005 IBM sold its last personal computer activities to the Chinese company Lenovo. A few years earlier, Siemens had already conceded its personal computer activities to a joint venture with Fujitsu.

The essential factor in a stable market-splitting niche strategy is not only the scale effects that a niche fighter can enjoy when it focuses on a subset of the value chain, but also the customer requirements. It will be increasingly difficult for the former scale leaders and global consolidators to satisfy customer requirements as specifically as a highly specialized competitor can.

9. COUNTER NICHES

Global consolidators are almost always market leaders—or so they tell themselves. Hungry Endgame niche fighters, on the other hand, often have a different perception. They recognize that pride of position often leads to myopic or irrational thinking, even with the most talented global consolidator. In the absence of the competitive pressure that is standard in the early phases of Merger Endgame consolidation, in which acquiring scale is paramount, the power of size hides many defects. Even in the Focus Phase, global consolidators can create a lot of value by working internally to reengineer processes and align competing demands on scarce resources. Sometimes even the internal politics of the burgeoning global consolidator creates a false reality.

Overall, the biggest risk that global consolidators face is that they may lose touch with their customers and begin to listen to their own ideas about how the market should work instead of the customers'. This usually marks the beginning of a notable decline in a company's innovative response to the marketplace. A recently published study from Harvard Business School revealed what we already know—that companies that dominate their markets tend to lose their innovativeness.

The list of former global leaders that have fallen victim to this kind of arrogance is long: General Motors, Ford, IBM, Alcoa, Daimler, Deutsche Bank, Bayer Leverkusen, Kodak, Unilever, Grundig, Sony, Coca-Cola, AT&T, and Allianz. Because of their excellent market position, all of these companies at one time or another exchanged reacting quickly to market pressure and ever-changing customer requirements for the pursuit of something else. It is difficult to name the "something else." "Status quo" comes to mind, or "linear continuation." But what feels like running forward is sometimes more like Wile E. Coyote already 30 feet off the cliff. Justification replaces insight, analysis trumps synthesis, and even the most powerful market leader begins to fall prey to its own mythologies. Because market insights are at odds with the trajectory of the business, targets such as quarterly earnings, share price, or other internal measures take precedence. The hungry counter niche fighter looks to find the customer segments that may be increasingly dissatisfied with the offer of the global consolidator.

A good example of this dreadful behavior is provided by General Motors in the last decades of the twentieth century. Formerly the leading manufacturer in the global automobile market, GM in 1980 still had a relative market share of 2—meaning twice as much as the next competitor. But since the 1960s, GM had been managed almost entirely by financial controllers. Share losses in the U.S. domestic market resulting from a completely antiquated product range were only part of the problem. In the counter niche opportunity created by the myopic GM, the Japanese and European producers developed a range of counter niche fighter strategies: Toyota, Nissan, Honda, and Mazda entered the lower-middle-class segment with high-quality and reasonably priced family cars; and the German manufacturers were convincing with their high-tech, high-speed luxury sedans. GM has recently responded with a portfolio of vehicles that better matches customer needs. But the counter niche fighters have staked their claim and now enjoy a stable niche position.

Ford has shown comparable weaknesses. It is reasonable to ask at this point in time whether there will still be a place for U.S. cars in the future, now that Daimler has sloughed off its ill-fated dalliance with Chrysler. The past strongly suggests that GM and Ford will dramatically change their positions in the market, with correspondingly dramatic changes in the U.S. industrial structure that will reach far beyond the automotive industry. All of these developments were created by a lack of flexibility, indifference to service, unimpressive innovation, and the previously mentioned arrogance of the established market leaders. The long-term impact may be that the old global consolidators are unseated and replaced with counter niche fighters.

Coca-Cola also seemed to take its eye off the ball at one point. Only about two decades ago, the soft-drink giant had a market share of 47 percent and appeared to be unassailable by its long-time competitor, Pepsi. After a misguided brand management policy in which Coke tampered with its traditional recipe, there was a surprising backlash. Coke's attempts to stretch its brand at the time, with New Coke versus Classic Coke, led many to think that it was losing touch with its core consumers. Perhaps more importantly, Coke failed to pick up on changing consumer tastes and new preferences for healthier beverage options, evident in the trend toward high-quality mineral waters. Coca-Cola lost its market position—even in the United States. In the market gaps that opened as a result, Nestlé, Danone, and the cooperative French mineral water suppliers pursued a counter niche strategy. These counter niche fighters achieved market leadership in the mineral water sector as the market demand for healthier beverage alternatives grew. Anyone who attends a business meeting in Beijing today will be struck by the fact that there is an ample supply of mineral water from Nestlé or Danone around the conference table. Only 10 years ago, Coca-Cola was the expression of the Western lifestyle. This shift can be attributed as much to the excellent marketing efforts of the water suppliers as to the lack of action on the part of Coca-Cola. In its complacency, this company became more and more stagnant and is now the "former market leader" in many beverage segments.

Entire national economies can fall into the slumber of market leadership. This presents counter niche opportunities for other national economies to penetrate these markets. In fact, this is one of the drivers of global consolidation as described by the Merger Endgame. For example, the economic miracle in the Federal

Republic of Germany that resulted from its post-World War II restructuring instilled a deep arrogance in a number of important industry sectors until far into the 1970s. The chemical, pharmaceutical, banking, insurance, machine tooling, and photography industries, as well as large parts of the automobile industry and large parts of the German brewery industry, all suffered from this myopia.

After 1970, Germany, Inc. began to struggle with this industrial self-satisfaction, developing an apparent indifference to service, and became stagnant as a result. This was exacerbated by the increasingly broad social support provisions of the social democratic political environment. By the 1990s, the results were obvious: German virtues of tenacity, dedication, and continuity that had received worldwide recognition gave way to myopia and a dismissive attitude toward service. Old truths rapidly reversed into myths. Deutsche Bank and Dresdner Bank lost their worldwide leadership positions. Hoechst, primarily because of Aventis's merger with the smaller company Sanofi-Synthélabo in France, lost its leading position in the pharmaceutical industry. And Allianz, which until 15 years ago was the leading insurance company in the world, is now in the relatively midrange in terms of market capitalization.

Today, France struggles contentiously with the growing power of foreign competition; Great Britain frets; Italy teeters on the brink. Eastern Europe faces imminent collapse. The United States presses forward on the strength of its significantly larger installed base— but with trillions of dollars of sovereign reserves in the hands of non-U.S. governments, it is only a matter of time before some ambitious new competitor overtakes it. For business strategists with an eye on 2020, the epochal shift—the global Endgame—has begun.

About 20 years ago, Unilever was nearly unapproachable both in the foodstuffs sector and in washing machines and body-care products. The management principles created at Unilever became well-known case studies, taught by international business schools and revered throughout the business world. Unilever was a benchmark for efficiency and effectiveness across industries worldwide.

In the foodstuffs sector, the far more aggressive Nestlé and Kraft Foods have driven out Unilever. Procter & Gamble and Beiersdorf have overtaken in the body-care sector, and Procter & Gamble has also taken over the laundry sector. While the regenerative power of Unilever should not be underestimated, the recently announced divestiture of its U.S. laundry business is a true indicator of the impact of these trends.

IBM is yet another former market leader that was previously thought unassailable. In the 1980s, IBM enjoyed a market share of 60 percent. With a complete IT product range, IBM was the epitome of an impenetrable market leader and seemed to dominate the future technology industry, with no competitors in sight. Thomas J. Watson's success story in creating tremendous shareholder value dominated the media and created an enormous buzz in business schools. IBM moved with great self-confidence and enjoyed legendary recognition in commercial and social circles. Fast forward to 2007: IBM, with a market capitalization of $138 billion, is only an average-performing stock in the Dow Jones. No longer is IBM a peer to the power players Microsoft, Oracle, SAP, Dell, or . . . even Apple. After the difficult but successful reorganization by Louis V. Gerstner, Jr., and in the days after 2002 when Samuel J. Palmisano took over, IBM is now in the process of rethinking even its hardware offerings and is increasingly becoming a service company—not a bad thing, but not IBM, global consolidator and market leader.

The strong positions of established market leaders, therefore, can be defended only if these companies maintain their superior performance levels and respond to internal and external pressure to innovate. They must also continually respond to ever-changing customer demands, which can result in new markets or newly defined markets. In essence, they must be an innovation niche or market-splitting fighter against themselves. General Electric is probably the only company to do this in the past 10 to 15 years. Despite tremendous success in almost all of its markets, GE has never stopped responding to pressure to perform and innovate. Even today, GE is better positioned both in innovative business areas such as China and India and in sustainable industries than most of its "small and nimble" competitors.

What conclusions can be drawn that will help emerging companies that want to create new market segments and serve them as stable Endgame niche fighters? When considering a niche strategy, a company must complete an in-depth examination of the strengths and weaknesses of the dominant suppliers in its target market. A company must also continually assess how well its own offering meets the current market as well as the new market sector it is considering. At the same time, companies need as much understanding as possible of the success factors and general issues affecting the industry, as well as the factors that have led to success in similar industries. As this knowledge is developed, it should be integrated into the corresponding strategy of the future niche fighter.

Building on this example, a company's counter niche strategy should be executed initially without being noticed, but with aggression and speed, exploiting the weaknesses of the market leaders. A counter niche fighter must also achieve relative scale advantages as soon as possible, to be able to build brand loyalty as customer relationships develop. Nobody wants to be a great little company with a superior product that got run over by a global consolidator.

Chapter Eight | How to Find and Structure an Endgame Niche

Niches receive a lot of attention, but few companies really think about the underlying structure and key success drivers of a stable Endgame niche. The overwhelming majority of companies can be defined as niche companies, but most of them do not seem to be sufficiently aware of the fact that their reason for being is inherently unstable over the next five to seven years. There is constant talk of industrial consolidation on the national, continental, and global levels. There is also commentary and lively discussion about the next big merger: Who will "get" whom? Who will become the next global consolidator—a company that once was innovative and fun, but now is just grinding through the sector to create scale advantage? Which companies will be the primary vehicles for implementing the consolidation process and moving it further along, thus making fears—or hopes—come true?

The final step that companies must take when considering an overall and global industry Endgame has so far been taken by only a few players. This is why the Alcan story in the previous chapter is so noteworthy. What steps must a company take when it is third or fourth in the market and has an unfavorable Endgame position? How can companies structure a successful long-term niche strategy? What should a company do if it thought it was a market leader, but someone has redefined its market? Or worse, what can a company do if it thought it was a global consolidator, but has had to concede its position because of a competitor's actions or its own inaction? Niche fighters are not just spunky little start-ups. They are also multibillion-dollar players that find themselves caught between those spunky little start-ups and the true global consolidators.

In our experience, there are six steps that a company needs to work through to stabilize its thinking about what Endgame niche strategy—if any—is going to prove helpful to the company's survival in the face of the onslaught of global consolidation. These six steps must be taken in order, as they build on each other. The process starts with understanding the Merger Endgame position of the industry sector, and ends with either a stable Endgame niche design or a logical sequence of integrated Endgame niches that extend stability through several phases of the Endgame.

SIX STEPS TO DEVELOPING A STABLE NICHE STRATEGY

Step 1: *Determine your industry's Endgame position, the strategic implications of that position, and the expected evolution of the industry's consolidation in the next five to ten years.*

Understanding which Merger Endgame phase an industry sector is in is key to developing a stable Endgame niche strategy. The strategic implications connected with each Endgame phase give the first indication of the degrees of freedom and the regulations of the industry sector. During a large part of the Scale Phase, future market leaders or global consolidators are just coming into their own. Thus, in the Opening Phase and, to a large extent, the Scale Phase, all niche strategy options are available.

Even in these Endgame phases, visionary entrepreneurs need to consider the future Endgame and their positioning as a stable Endgame niche fighter in detail. Does it make sense to forge ahead into regional, product, or target-group niches, albeit prematurely, just to stay above the wave of global consolidation, as Reliance and Aditya Birla are doing with billions of dollars of investment in India? Or should the concentration be on speed segments or lightning consolidations to challenge the former market leaders for their leading positions? As soon as companies can predict their industry's behavior—at least, as accurately as possible—they can begin to formulate a plan that will allow them to navigate the Merger Endgame, whether as a niche fighter, a global consolidator, or a cash-out king. In many ways, this has to be the ultimate and only objective of any corporate strategy.

Step 2: *Identify industry sectors with comparable consolidation models that are at a later phase of the Endgame. Use these models to illuminate the Endgame and identify strategic success factors for your own industry sector.*

Companies can project the Endgame for their own industry sector by gleaning lessons from other comparable sectors. This will enable them to better forecast their best strategic moves. For example, it's uncanny how the steel industry's current Endgame matches that of the aluminum industry five years earlier. Only a few years ago, Alcan merged with Pechiney and, with its very successful organic growth, was able to compete closely with the market leader, Alcoa. In the Value Building Growth matrix, Alcoa had been losing its position to Alcan for some time. This sector's Endgame is the model for the steel market.

Mittal Steel's lightning consolidation of the steel industry was certainly a takeover maneuver from an initially weak niche position. It is likely that this model will be repeated in other metal and mining sectors. The Endgame stories for 180 industry sectors in the Value Building Growth matrix are a rich resource for deriving such model examples. Based on empirical information, these stories provide clear insights that can stimulate and encourage executives to rethink their future profit-making potential.

Step 3: *Decide who the Endgame consolidation winners and losers are and know their strengths and weaknesses inside and out.*

Knowing an industry's market structure, its segmentation, and the anticipated changes in its segments over time is extremely important when evaluating niche options. Will the sector explode into segment diversity, like the IT industry? Or will it implode, as the pharmaceutical industry has done? Or is the industry so driven by scale advantage that Endgame consolidation is accelerated by agglomeration, as in retail?

Finding these models and predicting future developments is very helpful in deriving stable Endgame niche strategies. Very often the failure of a niche strategy can be traced back to a fundamental misinterpretation of the Endgame environment. Equally important is analyzing an industry's value-creation structure in terms of how it breaks down into individual elements and how these elements are reintegrated. Will the value chain recombine in a new way, as was seen in the IT industry when IBM disintegrated into mainframes, microcomputers, IT services, chips, software, and even microsoftware? Or are the scale effects of the global consolidators so strong that they can simply overrule segment differences, as we have seen in retail, with the integrated scale effects dominating in purchasing, systems, and branding?

Step 4: *Analyze the industry sector's market and segment structure and the value-creation structure to identify potential market splits and new configurations for the value-creation chain.*

Players in the global consolidation race will generally surface at the end of the Scale Phase. If their strategic and operational histories are considered, it is fairly easy to determine whether these players will successfully complete the march to the top. The victims of consolidation are also recognizable at the end of the Scale Phase.

As for the emerging global consolidators, their strengths and weaknesses provide specific opportunities that niche fighters can exploit. When Big American Steel was pounding out pigs and ingots, Japanese Steel crept into the U.S. market and seized a market position with bent, rolled, crimped, and any other kind of high-service content customers might have wanted. This was precisely the strategy that Alcan used, concentrating on processing to compete with the market leader Alcoa, which prided itself on being a pure raw material supplier.

And it's certainly no surprise that most European retail groups have somehow become more hyperresponsive to consumers' national interests. Mercator in Slovenia and El Corte Inglés in Spain are two examples that come to mind. Wal-Mart didn't have anything to do with that, did it? Perhaps the best example is still Tesco and ASDA, Wal-Mart's subsidiary in the United Kingdom. Tesco, the local Endgame niche fighter, gave Wal-Mart as good as it got in a denim jeans price war, which ended in a standoff at about $8 a pair, with everybody (except the shopper) having lost money. But in this case, the niche fighter (Tesco is technically still an Endgame niche fighter) had beaten the global consolidator.

Step 5: *Determine the best niche options and determine the best sequence for executing them.*

The right options are hard to find. After the Bancroft family publicly fumbled the sale of Dow Jones in 2007, the Ford family met a few months later to discuss their options in the event of a similar situation. The best way to find a good option is to look at a lot of bad ones and understand why they failed. Most unsuccessful entrepreneurs don't fail because their idea wasn't good; they fail because their idea wasn't better than the other available options. This is not meant to be a trite statement.

The life cycle of businesses rarely extends unchanged for more than 50 years, and the life cycle of birth to death or substantial rejuvenation is shortening. GE is a great example. Its atavistic strategy of growth and destruction allowed executives at this venerable giant operating in more than a dozen industry sectors to state calmly in 2007 that the subprime credit problem in the United States didn't worry them. GE's future prospects from India and China and sustainable industries far outweighed any concerns it might have had in that area.

If companies can find an Endgame niche strategy that is stable for five to seven years, with a prospect of connecting it to a related stable Endgame niche strategy for another five to seven years and then linking it to a third, they have struck gold. If the company owners can then cap it all off by selling out to a global consolidator and buying that house on Capri, all the better. Or if the owners can buy the global consolidator and become the new king of the mountain, that's even better—the competitor gets the house on Capri, but the new leader has another seven years. Maximizing a company's value is an important part of the Endgame niche strategy process, but maximizing the period of survival is what is really important.

Step 6: *Select and elaborate the optimal niche with regard to its appropriate time frame.*

Successful Endgame niche strategies aren't a dime a dozen, but they're also not one in a million. Based on our empirical research, they are more likely one in 200,000. A great strategy describes what customers a company will serve with what kind of product or service and in what way. More importantly, it describes what the company will not do, something that most failed companies do not fully consider.

It is equally important to test a strategy against the facts and to reevaluate that strategy based on reality. In the late 1990s, we were asked by an industry association to do an industry-sector horizon scan for its members—U.S. food wholesalers and distribution companies that were mostly family-owned, regional players. Our conclusions were pretty simple: "Prepare your companies for sale, so that your children will have more money." Despite the barrage of claims to the contrary, the consolidation of food wholesalers in the United States continues at a rapid pace.

As we've shown throughout this book, however, not every industry sector is as scale-crazy as food wholesalers in the United States. There are numerous sectors to play and fight in—and if you didn't believe that, you wouldn't have read this far.

It goes without saying that the stable niche fighter should be even more vigilant than the global consolidator when meeting with customers, understanding how segments are changing, and reading and keeping informed about all aspects of the sector and its business. It may sound silly, but when you feel like David up against Goliath, sometimes you forget to put a second rock in your pocket. We have already discussed how global consolidators can get complacent, leaving big openings for counter niche fighters that, like Don Quixote, have a dream that is unrelated to what's happening in their industry sector and fight on, fighting the impossible fight undeterred by rebuffs from customers and competitors alike.

Experience shows that to secure such concepts, it is necessary to check them on a regular basis in qualified marketing meetings and client interviews and to constantly check individual results. This also applies to the involvement of industry consultants and other specialists on the technical side—experts who are used by many successful companies. It is only the combination of elements from the community, client, and market that leads to an appropriate target-oriented strategy, which in the end provides the angle for the derivation of a successful Endgame niche approach.

Chapter Nine | The Unexploited Potential of the Endgame Niches

The countless managers who find out to their surprise that their company is active in a niche whose window of opportunity is already coming to an end must use new strategic approaches to position themselves in the old and new markets with old and new clients. A simple matrix of standardized strategies for those companies that are presently in Endgame niches, but can already foresee the Endgame, will not be considered here. Standard procedures are by definition not strategies, because each individual case is different and therefore demands different targets and priorities. The initial situation, the parameters of the competition, the technology, and the regional emphasis all offer different roads to the objective—not only for each industry, but also for each company.

The investigation of the 600 companies, filtered from the worldwide universe of companies, that have survived the past 15 years as Endgame niche fighters has led to a series of far-reaching results that places the application of the nine Endgame niche strategies in their broader context:

- The identified niches do not apply in the same way to all industries—there are clear industry-specific emphases.
- Endgame niche strategies frequently occur as combinations. Approximately 83 percent of the niche companies studied have not concentrated on a single niche, but use the protection of several niche parameters. These combinations, however, do not occur in constant clusters, so that while correlations can be derived, they vary strongly from one another.
- The available arsenal of potential Endgame niches is used in different ways. The niche variants in the late phases of the Endgame curve have particularly low frequencies, which leads us to hypothesize that substantial unexploited opportunities for many companies still exist in this area.

INDUSTRY-SPECIFIC EMPHASIS

All of the Endgame niches described in this book have equally "natural" industry-sector affinities. This means that there are industries in which some niches are occupied more frequently than others. It also means that certain specific niche forms can grow very successfully in some industries, but not so well in others. There are numerous interesting examples. For example, the combination of the target-group niche and the branding niche—not an unexpected combination—appears predominant in fast-moving consumer goods and other consumer-related sectors, and indeed to some extent is clearly overrepresented in some of these sectors (see Figure 9-1).

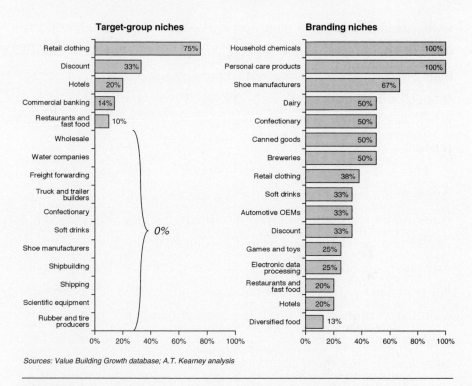

Figure 9-1. Frequency of target-group and branding niche strategies by industry

An orientation toward clearly defined target groups and the use of a strong brand characterize the strategy of these companies. And, in the case of NIVEA, this strategy has led to substantial success.

However, this by no means suggests that this combination has the greatest potential for success. Bringing in elements of product niche and innovation niche strategies would possibly have made the "strategy bundle" even more successful. The rise of BMW suggests this.

Some companies concentrate on branding and target-group proximity, but also include other parameters. Molkerei Alois Müller, for example, could be regarded as extremely innovative in its own areas. In the industries mentioned, there are clear tendencies to combine the branding and target-group niche strategies. Certainly, even for companies that are not in the consumer goods industries, this combination is worth considering. Every day each of us has a genuine consumer experience that could probably inform our business' strategy.

Our study shows that only 17 percent of companies appear as "pure niche types," and 83 percent involve combinations. These combinations are not specific to industry sectors, and they don't cluster in a way that allows us to draw deeper conclusions from their existence. It could be that not enough empirical work such as ours has been done. Thus there are no fixed combinations that can form a strategic "unit." However, it is apparent that more complex combinations are demonstrably more successful than others and that companies using them remain in the upper right quadrant of the Value Building Growth matrix for a longer time before either losing momentum and becoming underperformers or concentrating too much on cost cutting and, as profit seekers, no longer finding a connection to healthy growth in value. The "simple growth" variant, which can be translated to "growth at any price," is not very present in the strong combinations of different niches.

Here we see, once again, the basic pattern of niche formation: The more "components" included in the Endgame niche formation, the better the niche can be defended, and therefore the more successful the niche strategy.

In the target-group/branding niche combination, this is apparent immediately. Tchibo is a great example. This coffee-shop chain brings in its faithful customers every week with the promise that they will find something new on the shelves as they sip their tasty espressos: The company's slogan is "every week a new world." Tchibo likes to say that its algorithm is very simple—manage thousands of new products in thousands of locations with a new assortment every week of the year, and with specials and promotions that are one time only for a target group that Tchibo understands better than anyone else. Just let Wal-Mart try to take this company out of business.

Not every target group/branding niche fighter is as aggressive as Tchibo. But why not also include product differentiation to make your position that much stronger? The prevalence of product niche and innovation niche combinations is also obvious. But why do so few companies include a cooperation or counter component in their niche formation, especially given the better position this would afford?

There is an abundance of unused potential waiting to be exploited by courageous and inventive entrepreneurs for the benefit of the customer and the macroeconomy. The large, "saturated" market leaders are not the companies that can still stimulate the economy. Stimuli come primarily from intelligently structured and constantly rethought niche companies that can creatively exploit their position and never wallow in supposed niche security.

COURAGE AND IDEAS ARE HELPFUL FOR SURVIVAL

On the basis of the study, a wide frequency distribution of the Endgame niches—recognizing that each niche fighter might be using two or even three distinct Endgame niche strategies—is apparent. No immediate conclusions can be drawn from this. The economy is heterogeneous, and so are niches. On second thought, however, it is possible to draw some very interesting conclusions from this context, since the "simpler," more obvious niche forms are clearly predominant (see Figure 9-2).

Most niche fighters are in a territory where few others could enter and maintain themselves very well, if they even noticed the niche possibility at all. This happens all the time. Entrepreneurs who have not done their homework move into these niches and do not fully exploit their strategic possibilities. The use of simple niche forms at least suggests too little differentiation in the market, therefore exposing a company to the risk that its products and services will easily be copied. Such niches will therefore be hard to defend in the long term.

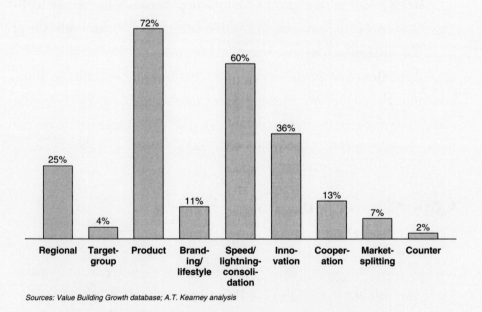

Sources: Value Building Growth database; A.T. Kearney analysis

Figure 9-2. Frequency distribution of niche strategies

The more complex forms of niches offer the best potential for survival and success. These forms include the cooperation, market-splitting, and counter niches. They are more difficult to apply and are as hard to find as to maintain, and therefore they are substantially underrepresented. Companies can only be advised to cultivate and nurture such niches in the long term to profit as much as possible from this choice of direction. For example, many new niche fighters are embracing cutting-edge technology and exploiting the emerging culture of social networks such as MySpace and Facebook, which are revolutionizing consumers' ability to evaluate and offer feedback on suppliers' competitive strategies. As with differentiated value-chain capabilities of the more prosaic variety, the success or failure of these new efforts depends strongly on distinguishing between what these technologies bring to the playing field and how they equalize the players versus what these technologies offer to distinguish the niche fighter permanently (or at least durably).

Let's get back, in this context, to the subject of worldwide industrial consolidation, which is the key existential threat for niches. In principle, niche players will, because of their smaller size, become victims of the Endgame. This means that they will be easily absorbed or must disappear from the market. The defenders of well-defended—or more complex and demanding—niches are better able to match the market leaders because of their distinguishing characteristics.

In view of the dramatic nature of global industrial consolidation and the scale of the companies affected by it, these are at least partly comforting findings. The money for hard-working and energetic entrepreneurs is still literally at our fingertips. But we have to keep grabbing and scratching to get it. A few points before we go:

- There are a large number of companies that, despite their relatively small size, can defeat the Endgame because of the stability of their Endgame niche.
- There are numerous possibilities for the formation of successful Endgame niches for those companies that analyze the market and the competitive environment intelligently.
- The potential is substantial—and not even remotely exploited.

Let's get going!

Chapter Ten | Tales from the Front: 15 Niche Fighter Stories

The summary insights from our Merger Endgames study lead us to view these Endgame niche horizons as truly exciting and challenge opportunities. But real success depends on specific market requirements and processes. As you read through the following case studies, we know they will resonate, perhaps reminding you of something you should have done three years ago—or what you are thinking of just now. By next year, these stories may be overtaken by other best examples—so read quickly and act fast (perhaps the best advice from any good business tome this year)!

Case Study 1

COSMOTE: Ringing Success in a Regional Niche

COSMOTE, a mobile telephone supplier, is a surprising regional triumph. As the third entrant into the Greek market, the company faced stiff competition from both Vodafone and TIM Hellas. However, COSMOTE was able to capitalize on its marketing expertise and the established network of its parent company, Hellenic Telecommunications Organization (OTE), to achieve rapid success. In just five years, COSMOTE passed its top two competitors and captured 37 percent of the Greek mobile telephone market. Today, more than 4 million customers use the company's services.

COSMOTE is a perfect example of a regional niche player. These players often derive their competitive advantage from their ability to determine the unique needs and behaviors of customers in their region and then deliver superior customer service. Regional niche players often establish more loyal relationships with customers because they have more nuanced and detailed information about what their customers require and desire. This can pose a formidable barrier to entry for global competitors, even when the regional player's products are priced higher.

Still, a regional niche player's advantages do not guarantee it protection from the global consolidators. Loyal customers can be lured away by cheaper products and a global brand. So far this has not been an issue for COSMOTE. The company has been able to defend its regional niche, in part by being uniquely able to serve customers in a geographic landscape that poses particularly dicey risks to most mobile telephone suppliers. COSMOTE successfully provides service to Greece's numerous islands and resolves quality issues with its network quickly—costly features that are less attractive to the global consolidators in this sector. At present, the company's network covers 95 percent of Greece's total landscape and 97 percent of its territorial waters.

This regional player's success can also be attributed to its marketing strategy. COSMOTE made large promotional investments that deliberately targeted Greek national pride. Like its parent company OTE, COSMOTE incorporated the Greek national colors of blue and white into its logo. The firm also recognized the unique opportunity to raise its profile during the 2004 Olympic Games in Athens. Before the start of the games, COSMOTE increased its service outlets throughout the Olympic Village, boosted its targeted ad campaigns, and added more athletes to its sponsorship roster. COSMOTE also used this opportunity to cleverly exploit other advantages of OTE's retail network, including taking over a chain of OTE retail shops and establishing 12 flagship branches in major Greek cities. With the Olympics as a launching pad, COSMOTE has since developed a network of more than 500 sales outlets, not only increasing its visibility throughout Greece but also offering more points of sale.

More recently, the firm has established a partnership with Levi Strauss to launch the first-ever Levi Mobile Phone collection, which targets a younger generation of consumers. The product will be sold at GERMANOS chain stores throughout Greece, further increasing COSMOTE's points of sale—and helping it to migrate from its successful regional niche strategy to a target-group niche strategy, which should prove more stable in the long term.

The success of COSMOTE's strategies can be seen in the numbers. The company's average annual revenue growth for the 2002–2006 period stands at 20.8 percent, compared to the industry average of only 8 percent. In addition, the firm has been able to capture 35 percent more contract customers than its closest competitor, Vodafone. Contract customers are preferred to prepaid customers because they ensure a steady flow of revenues in the short to medium term.

As COSMOTE seeks new customers, it knows that it must continue to deliver a high level of service and creative marketing. Results from other regions indicate that it is meeting these objectives. In 2007, COSMOTE subsidiary AMC added 1 million subscribers to its roster, becoming the market leader in the Albanian mobile telecommunications market.

Finally, as a new CEO and CFO take the helm, COSMOTE must maintain its momentum. It remains unclear whether changes at the top will alter what has so far been an enormously successful company. But COSMOTE's track record of identifying and executing stable Endgame niche strategies increases its chances of surviving the consolidation of the telecom sector.

Case Study 2

MERCATOR: THE REGIONAL NICHE WELL SOLD

Another regional niche success story is the Mercator Group, a major retail chain in Slovenia. Mercator was losing money hand over fist until 1997. But by 2004, the company had acquired a leading position in Slovenia. Despite deteriorating market conditions, Mercator was able to develop a regional retail niche and use its success as a catalyst for further expansion.

Much of Mercator's success is the result of a regional niche strategy. Mercator understood the importance of the positive customer perception generated by selling local products and brands in Slovenia (and later also in the markets of the adjoining countries), and the need for close collaboration between local manufacturers and retailers.

From 1997 onward, Mercator pursued a development strategy to reverse the negative trends of the preceding years and positioned itself as the top retailer in the country (catching up to the leading retail chains in Europe and around the world). To accomplish this, management took several far-reaching measures: The company pursued an internal restructuring; integrated the Slovenian food manufacturers; accelerated the growth of its retail network and marketing activities; acquired retailers in Slovenia, Croatia, and Bosnia and Herzegovina to increase scale; and penetrated new markets by establishing new subsidiaries in these countries. By 2004, Mercator was growing through acquisitions, developing its greenfield stores, and pursuing a highly effective marketing campaign.

Mercator's retail portfolio is now composed of four different segments: grocery, hardware and electronics, textile and beauty, and sports. In addition, Mercator has a wholesale business and produces a wide array of its own items, including kitchen accessories, jams, frozen foods, cocoa, and coffee. The company is also developing a service segment, which includes hotels, restaurants, and canteens.

Mercator has tailored both its products and its store formats to meet relevant regional needs. As of 2006, Mercator had a total of six primary store formats: 362 superettes, 156 supermarkets, 113 neighborhood stores, 39 hypermarkets, 14 hard discount stores, and 9 cash-and-carry stores. Additionally, Mercator operated furniture stores, clothing stores, restaurants, and other specialty formats.

In the past five years, Mercator has focused its growth on new regional markets such as Croatia, Serbia, and Bosnia and Herzegovina. Sales in these new markets were responsible for more than 20 percent of total revenues in 2006, a 50 percent increase over the previous year. These countries have significant growth potential in retail as a result of anticipated economic expansion.

Different countries require different approaches to retail. In Croatia, shops have been developed in both the major cities and tourist areas. In the economically weaker region of Bosnia and Herzegovina, most shops are in the major urban areas. Across these countries, Mercator has managed to skirt a series of obstacles, particularly those related to political and commercial instability. As Bosnia and Herzegovina regained stability, Mercator was right there with retail solutions when the global consolidators were waiting on the sidelines. Its unique capability to do so—while the global consolidators decided to stay out of the market for the time being—gives it a stable Endgame regional niche.

In the near future, Mercator will face still greater challenges as the hard discount retailers such as Lidl, ALDI, and Hofer enter the market. This will surely test the stability and sustainability of Mercator's regional niche. If Mercator can migrate from its current successful regional niche strategy and add components of a stable branding or target-group niche, it will be able to fend off consolidation for a few more years.

Case Study 3

BMW: SPORTY DRIVING FROM A PRODUCT NICHE

Since the 1950s, BMW has been serving an exclusive product and target-group niche. Bayerische Motoren Werke is positioned as the automobile manufacturer of sporty cars that fall somewhere between the high-priced manufacturers, such as Mercedes-Benz, and the medium-class segments, such as Opel and Ford.

In the immediate postwar era, BMW was in a downward spiral. The motorcycle branch was the only profitable division at the time, and losses from the automobile division were more than depleting these profits. BMW's salvation was the bubble car Isetta—a mixture of motorcycle and car that was successful because it met the needs of the time for cheap, economical, short-distance transport. In 1955, BMW took over the license to produce the Isetta. It was the first niche vehicle that the company produced, and it became the start of a long success story for BMW as a product niche player.

However, by 1962 the bubble-car craze was petering out and customers were looking for "normal" passenger cars. BMW turned its attention to developing mid-sized cars (because luxury autos were not yet a viable option) and recognized that its emphasis should be on mid-sized cars with a bent toward exclusivity and sportiness. In this way, BMW sought to distinguish its cars from the competition.

When Herbert Quandt acquired the majority of BMW at the end of the 1950s, he insisted that the price for the new model introduced in the early 1960s, the BMW 1500, should be 10 percent higher than that proposed by the board. This marked the first step in creating a product and target-group niche. Quandt wanted customers to feel that they were buying an exclusive product and, more importantly, he wanted them to be willing to pay a premium for owning such a product.

The strategy worked, hitting its stride under the leadership of Paul Hahnemann, who moved to BMW from Auto Union in 1961. Hahnemann deliberately built on this niche strategy by focusing on bigger engines and higher-quality cars and introducing a "new class" to the market. Hahnemann was soon dubbed "Niche Paul" by the motor press and his colleagues.

BMW was becoming a sporty alternative to Mercedes-Benz, Opel, and VW. The strength of BMW, coupled with the growth of this niche, enabled it to dwell alongside its once superior competitors. With the BMW model 2500, the predecessor of the present 5 Series, BMW started to compete with Mercedes-Benz directly—but as a peer, rather than as a come-from-behind contender.

Since then, changes in the BMW models have forced Mercedes-Benz to constantly adapt its design and technology. It's a safe assumption that the German car industry would not be as strong as it is today without this competition.

And, while the sporty niche strategy is now legendary and has been copied by numerous auto manufacturers, BMW has not stood still. BMW products have developed into a lifestyle accessory for the middle and upper classes. With the BMW brand, customers own not only a vehicle that gets them from one place to another rapidly, but also one that communicates a certain lifestyle, that of a successful professional who can afford luxury.

The strength of BMW's strategy has led to many recent successes. Net profit, a volatile measure for this company, grew by 28 percent in 2006, while revenue growth averaged 6 percent from 2004 to 2007. The company maintains an ambitious production schedule and is outselling its rival Volkswagen's Audi brand and Daimler's Mercedes-Benz car group division.

The BMW Group's continued success is largely due to the company's position as an Endgame product niche fighter, with elements of strong branding, product, and target-group strategies. It is among a handful of worldwide automobile manufacturers that pursue a pure premium brand strategy. All deviations from the brand have been less successful. For example, when the MINI was added to the brand, it was a strong product, but it did not fit BMW's niche image. The BMW automobile remains the company's flagship product, accounting for 80 percent of all sales worldwide.

Not content to rest on its laurels, BMW continues to build on its linchpin product with additional vehicles that target distinct segments. For example, in 2004, BMW proved many skeptics wrong when it released its 1 Series premium car in Europe. The company's smallest car, the 1 Series has succeeded where both the Audi A2 and the Mercedes-Benz B-Class cars have failed, becoming firmly established in Europe as BMW's number two seller (after the 3 Series), with 81,486 units sold in the first eight months. Still, the long-term success of the 1 Series remains in question, as profits are fairly thin. A BMW spokesperson says that the 1 Series boasts a 10 percent or greater profit margin, but analysts think the margin is closer to 2 or 3 percent. It also remains to be seen whether the 1 Series will be a hit in the North American market.

BMW has successfully distinguished itself from many of its competitors and is now entering the Scale Phase and a battle for dominance against Daimler and Audi. Now in the Endgame, and no longer protected by its niche, BMW will continue to be recognized for its design and quality performance while also expanding its core customer group. It should see smooth—and sporty—sailing in the turbulent auto sector.

Case Study 4

NETJETS: FLYING HIGH IN A TARGET-GROUP NICHE

Flying was a day-to-day event for Richard T. Santulli, as it was for countless other executives. And like other frequent flyers, Santulli resented spending time in so-called VIP lounges and waiting in long lines at airports. Desperate for an alternative, in 1986, Santulli considered purchasing a private jet. However, while the convenience and flexibility made sense, the finances didn't. He could not use the jet often enough to justify paying the maintenance costs on his own, and co-owning a jet with partners wouldn't work, as they all wanted to use the same jet at the same time. Santulli calculated various financial scenarios for the joint use of a private jet and came up with a completely new concept: the NetJets ownership model, which charges clients based on fractional ownership and usage.

NetJets offers its clients two ways to participate: (1) fractional aircraft ownership, in which participants own one-sixteenth of an aircraft and get 50 flying hours per year, or (2) a Marquis Jet Card, which allows clients 25 flying hours per year. Prices are fixed and are applied on an hourly basis, irrespective of whether the ticket is for one-way or round-trip travel. Compared to charter flights, a NetJets flight is substantially cheaper. NetJets also offers a "Fly Ferry Free" program, which waives ferry fees for flights to certain international destinations.

In 1998, impressed with the NetJets model, Warren Buffett bought the company, adding NetJets to the Berkshire

Hathaway portfolio and retaining Santulli as chairman. The company now has a global presence (in the United States, Europe, and the Middle East) and a fleet of more than 700 aircraft. Of the thousands of joint owners, more than half have joined NetJets since 1999. NetJets now sells more flight time than all other suppliers of aircraft sharing combined.

The primary market for NetJets's target-group niche is U.S. executives who demand the kind of exclusive service that a private jet offers, but for whom the cost of owning a private jet is usually prohibitive. Since these customers normally fly first or business class on commercial flights, they are accustomed to paying more for their flights.

The demand for private jets rose significantly after the attacks of September 11, 2001, fueled by heightened security measures at major airports that meant longer waiting times and other inconveniences that affected U.S. executives in particular.

NetJets offers a level of convenience that is not possible with traditional airlines. For example, NetJets's smaller planes do not require the long runways of major airports, so they can land at and depart from smaller regional airports that are usually more accessible. Check-in time at these airports is reduced or nonexistent.

In 1996, NetJets entered the European aviation market and within 10 years had more than 100 planes in its European fleet. Although the European market has developed more slowly than the U.S. market, mainly because of political and legal obstacles in Europe, the Endgame target-group niche strategy is proving to be as stable in Europe as it is in America. In 2005, NetJets Europe's figures were profitable for the first time, and the division became profitable overall in 2006.

With a stable target-group niche strategy, NetJets has secured a foothold in the highly competitive aviation market. The company continues to find creative ways to expand its customer base—for example, launching advertising promotions featuring Tiger Woods and Roger Federer. In addition, NetJets has formed a strategic alliance with Lufthansa to provide private jet service (Lufthansa Private Jet), which should allow it to expand its customer base without hurting its image. More recently, NetJets introduced the NetJets Climate Initiative to incorporate "green" business practices into the company's operations with a combination of emission-reduction and carbon-offset programs.

Case Study 5

GORENJE: SOLD-OUT SUCCESS IN THE INNOVATION NICHE

The Gorenje Group is one of the largest companies in Slovenia, with sales of more than $1.6 billion and almost 11,000 employees in 2006. As a major manufacturer of white goods (large household appliances), the company holds a 4 percent share of the European appliance market. Begun as a state-run company, which inherently gave it a regional niche in Southeastern and Eastern Europe, it was privatized in 1997 and has since sought to extend into an innovation niche by leveraging its R&D, speed to market, and low-cost manufacturing capabilities.

Gorenje boasts one of the highest growth rates in an industry characterized by low margins and slow growth. Between 1999 and 2006, the company increased its annual revenues by 10 percent and its production by almost 70 percent, manufacturing more than 3.5 million household goods. Gorenje maintains its regional advantage in Eastern and Southeastern Europe (mainly the former Yugoslavia), where the Gorenje name continues to be synonymous with refrigerators. More recently, the member states of the European Union (EU) have become its most important market; 57 percent of revenues were generated from sales to EU countries in 2006.

How did Gorenje survive the collapse of its major market, Yugoslavia? When Yugoslavia began to fall apart in the early 1990s, the company saw a 40 percent loss in sales. Gorenje's management decided to confront this crisis with various initiatives. It improved its R&D, technical expertise, and flexibility, allowing it to surpass its major competitors in the white-goods market in time to market. Today, Gorenje can conceive, develop and commercialize new products in an average of 12 months, well below the lead times of its larger competitors.

Furthermore, through the generous support of the company's banks and suppliers, all jobs were saved; this created a strong, loyal, and motivated workforce that worked with the company to reduce production costs and thus become more competitive.

From its geographic position in the Balkans, Gorenje has since pursued a two-pronged strategy. First, it exploits its regional niche by building and selling a broad and diverse range of products in the former Yugoslavia and Eastern Europe. Second, the company pursues a low-cost innovation niche by exporting innovative large household appliances at low prices to Western Europe.

Gorenje recognizes the importance of partnerships for improving critical elements of its value chain. For example, early in its history, the company pursued growth in EU countries by building partnerships in growing markets. A case in point is its decision in 1961 to supply German mail-order companies (such as Neckermann) with high-quality, reasonably priced products.

The company is again turning to a partnership strategy to strengthen its Endgame innovation niche strategy. To build its image as a design and technology trendsetter, and thus move into higher-priced markets, Gorenje has formed a partnership with the award-winning Italian design studio Pininfarina. The Pininfarina design line of Gorenje household goods not only is beautiful but also incorporates advanced-technology touch-control sensors, replacing mechanical knobs on appliances.

With these initiatives, the Slovenian white-goods manu-facturer and stable Endgame regional, innovation, and—increasingly—brand niche fighter plans to pursue more defined innovation niches and increase its market share in the competitive European market.

Case Study 6

SWATCH: TIMING THE RIGHT MOVE FROM ONE NICHE STRATEGY TO ANOTHER

In the 1970s, the Swiss watchmakers SSIH and ASUAG struggled as the watch market was flooded with cheaper brands from Japan and Hong Kong that relied on quartz technology. In 1983, both companies faced the threat of bankruptcy and were advised to merge, forming what is now dubbed the Swatch Group. At this point, Swatch staged a dramatic turnaround.

What Swatch achieved during the 1980s was nothing short of a revolution in the watch market. Despite objections that the company's high-quality, premium brand might be ruined, the new Swatch Group introduced its first low-cost watch to the Swiss market. The Swatch watch was an instant success and became a pop-culture icon of the 1980s. After just two years on the market, Swatch watches were being sold on every continent, with sales reaching a staggering $5.4 billion in 2007.

At the other end of the product range, traditional Swiss watches went from being viewed as standard accessories to being seen as luxury items. Swatch, seeking to capitalize on this, in 1992 purchased Blancpain, a luxury watch manufacturer, and Frédéric Piguet, a luxury watch components manufacturer. These acquisitions allowed Swatch to compete and lead in a number of market segments. With 18 watch brands across all segments—from entry level to luxury—Swatch is able to offset weaknesses in one segment with increased sales in another.

Swatch also differentiated itself from the market through its production and R&D expertise. From the Swatch Group's early beginnings, R&D investments have been crucial to its success. For instance, 200 employees worked for almost two years to develop its low-cost model, spending almost $9 million in R&D. Also, the Swatch Group invests heavily in its in-house manufacturing capabilities and thus, unlike its competitors, can develop and manufacture all of its own designs.

This in-house capability is invaluable as the company adapts to meet consumer demand. For example, as mechanical-movement watches have become more popular, Swatch controls 65 percent of the market. As a result, it can stay ahead of new innovations, capture revenues by acting as a supplier to competing watchmakers, and, in the process, gain market intelligence.

Swatch also uses its in-house capabilities to bring more ambitious models to the market. The company has developed collections designed by famous contemporary artists, including Keith Haring, Kiki Picasso, and Pierre Alechinsky. Gradually, it has created various formats and additional series, including innovations such as the Pop Swatch, the Maxi Swatch, the Scuba 200, and the Chronograph. Prices for these special editions are substantially higher than those for standard products, leading to the creation of a niche within a niche—the young collector.

Before Swatch developed collector's editions for a younger target audience, watch collecting belonged almost exclusively to the wealthy, who often passed timepieces down as family heirlooms. Swatch collectors, on the other hand, are motivated by entirely different things: reasonable prices, intense marketing, and trendy designs.

Swatch uses its unique design and marketing to create a lifestyle brand that identifies with pop culture, thereby driving up sales even further. Swatch's stock has outperformed those of other companies in the luxury sector and was up 32 percent in the third quarter of 2007. By 2010, Swatch profits are expected to exceed those of its luxury competitors by almost 4 percent, or 17 percent versus 13 percent. In addition, in 2006, Swatch occupied the number one revenue position with $4 billion, while the same year Omega, among the three largest watch brands in the world, grossed a little more than $1 billion in sales.

Despite Swatch's tremendous success, challenges remain. For example, bottlenecks have prevented Swatch from keeping up with recent demand. Breguet, Swatch's number one luxury watch brand, may take more than a year to deliver. These bottlenecks are likely to worsen in 2008, when Swatch will be an official sponsor of the Olympic Games in Beijing. The delays in production underline a shortage of skilled labor, which threatens the company's stable Endgame niche.

Swatch has taken steps to deal with the shortage by establishing watch-training schools in China, Malaysia, the United Kingdom, and the United States. Swatch also plans to hire and train another 500 watchmakers.

The firm will also need to invest in its fixed assets, albeit cautiously, to maintain the flexibility needed to respond to any economic downturn that might slow customer demand. But, with more than 20 years of stellar financial performance and insightful management behind it, Swatch has demonstrated the ability to exploit stable Endgame niches and thus *keep on ticking*.

Case Study 7

ZARA: A PRODUCT NICHE STRATEGY WITH A FAST-FASHION TWIST

Fashion clothing retailer Zara, a subsidiary of the Spanish Inditex Group, enjoys a number of strategic advantages over its competitors. Inditex owns more than 50 percent of Zara's production capacity, has strong partnerships with local Spanish and Portuguese garment manufacturers (which provide additional production capacity), and owns almost all of the Zara retail shops worldwide. This high degree of vertical integration, coupled with transparent communications along the entire value chain, gives Zara the flexibility to respond quickly to market demands.

Zara occupies a clear product niche by stocking stores with up-to-the-minute fashions thanks to its near-total control of its value chain for fast-fashion items. Everything in the Zara value chain is designed to resist emulation by a competitor or a global consolidator. For example, the retail staff uses PDAs to upload the latest fashion trends and download inventory information. In-house design teams meet continually to monitor fashion trends around the world and immediately put them into production. Zara's wholly owned small-batch stitching rooms can turn out six weeks of inventory for a single store as easily as a much larger run.

While many competitors have long lead times because they outsource manufacturing to Asia to save costs, Zara produces high-fashion goods exclusively at its own production facilities. This allows Zara flexible manufacturing, effective communication, and increased speed to market. The only things Zara outsources to Asia are items such as undergarments and nonseasonal household accessories. This business model also allows Zara to monitor labor conditions in its manufacturing facilities, thus ensuring that the company does not receive negative press as a result of suboptimal factory conditions.

Zara's full control over its value chain means that it can design, manufacture, and sell new clothing faster than its competitors can. It takes Zara about four weeks to produce completely new designs, from conception to store inventory, compared to nine months for competitors (six months for design and three months for production). If Zara needs to modify an existing design, the redesigned products can arrive in stores within two weeks. This speed to market gives Zara the ability to meet up-to-the-minute consumer fashion demands.

The company produces new collections in small batches and tests them in both flagship and high-volume retail stores that cater to fashion trendsetters. If the test phase shows that some parts of the new collection are not meeting sales projections, adjustments in the color, cut, or style are made. By controlling its own value chain, the company can have modified products hanging in its shops again within a month. These "test runs" and the associated flexibility minimize overproduction of slow-selling lines. As a result, Zara has reduced the "flop rate" of its products to 1 percent, an amazing feat given that the industry average is about 10 percent.

Zara optimizes production capacity, resources, and costs and avoids having to sell lots of excess merchandise at a loss at the end of each season, which contributes to the positive brand image of the chain. The retailer's focus is not on producing large volumes of products for everyone, but rather on producing small quantities of products that meet the unique needs of its consumers. There are several benefits to this approach. For one thing, Zara holds little inventory, saving expensive warehousing and capital costs. Zara's customers gain more exclusivity in their clothing selections, as new and unique styles are constantly cycling through its stores. And by rapidly updating fashions in small batches, it drives more customer traffic. Fashion-conscious customers know that new goods are delivered often, and they visit Zara's shops frequently to purchase those goods before they are gone. The average Zara customer visits its retail stores 17 times per year, compared to a competitor's average of 4 visits per year. With such a loyal client base, Zara does not have to spend a lot on marketing. Its marketing budget amounts to 0.3 percent of sales compared to 3 to 4 percent of sales for competitors.

Zara's store-location strategy is also notable. The company selects real estate in high-traffic areas such as popular shopping districts and shopping malls but does not offset the high cost of its properties by stocking a large number of goods per square foot. Rather, the shops have an open layout, both to encourage customers to browse and to create a positive overall experience.

The retailer's value proposition has led to amazing financial growth and rapid geographic expansion. In 2006, Zara opened more than 200 shops worldwide, an average of almost four stores per week. The retailer reached an additional milestone in 2006 when it became Spain's number one independently owned brand, surpassing Hennes & Mauritz (H&M) as Europe's leading fashion retailer.

Although control of all design, warehouse, distribution, and logistics functions seems to go against current commercial logic, Zara has gained unique flexibility through this high degree of vertical integration. And while competitors have tried to match Zara's business and speed-to-market model by improving communication throughout their value chains, none has achieved the same results. "Fast fashion" not only has become a successful and stable Endgame product niche, but has also led to a cadre of target-group shoppers who visit a Zara store once every three weeks!

Case Study 8

ALCAN: FROM COUNTER NICHE TO GLOBAL CONSOLIDATOR . . . TO ENDGAME ACQUISITION

It is difficult to imagine how a company that primarily produces a "commodity" product could become a niche player in its industry. In recent years, however, Alcan has accomplished just that, becoming one of the largest aluminum and packaging companies in the world.

Alcan was initially positioned as a low-price aluminum production supplier. Because of its independent energy supply (50 percent versus the industry average of 25 percent), the company was able to sell aluminum at extremely low prices. This efficient use of resources is Alcan's core competence and explains how it has built a decisive competitive advantage against its rivals and was not bogged down in different stages of the value chain.

Alcan has leveraged its state-of-the-art R&D capabilities in core business areas, along with its collaboration with clients, suppliers, and other partners. The company's expansion of its aluminum-based packaging products branch was a deliberate strategy to position itself as a strong product niche fighter relative to Alcoa and other aluminum producers. This diverse product suite substantially reduced Alcan's sensitivity to price shifts and other economic factors.

In particular, Alcan is characterized by the complete set of packaging solutions it offers. It is the world market leader for flexible foodstuffs, pharmaceuticals, and cosmetics packaging, and is second in the area of tobacco packaging. Alcan is also one of the leading metal traders and producers of technology products and adhesives for the aviation, aeronautics, automobile, and beverage can industries. Customers from all of these industries make up a significant portion of Alcan's niche.

Alcan's growth has also been due to a lightning acquisition strategy in which it integrates target companies without incurring substantial long-term costs. Alcan streamlines the functions of the acquired companies to focus on core business areas—and quickly achieve synergies and therefore the value-creation potential. The result is a company with the most modern smelting technology that produces low-priced primary and progressive aluminum.

In late 2007, Alcan was acquired by Rio Tinto, a large U.K.-based mining company. The resulting company, Rio Tinto Alcan, is expected to become the world's largest aluminum producer, with a 15 percent market share. However, there are several major risks associated with this acquisition. To help offset the $46.3 billion in financing required for the purchase, Rio Tinto is expected to divest several of its acquired assets. One of those assets is the packaging division, which is a major factor that differentiates Alcan from its competitors.

Also under scrutiny is Alcan's engineering products group, described as "world class." In addition, as in all mergers and acquisitions, there is the potential for voluntary and involuntary attrition. A large exodus of Alcan's talent could severely damage the company's knowledge base, especially in critical R&D areas. Finally, if the integration of Rio Tinto and Alcan causes management to divert its attention from marketplace innovation, many of the gains of the past few years could disappear—and increased costs and inefficiencies may outweigh the benefits previously realized from its independent energy supply.

While Alcan has enjoyed a stable Endgame niche in the aluminum industry, it is again in uncharted waters—this time as Rio Tinto Alcan.

Case Study 9

DUCATI: KEEPING A STABLE BRANDING NICHE STRATEGY

In 1996, losses and cash-flow problems were mounting at Ducati, an Italian manufacturer of high-performance motorcycles. Suppliers could not be paid and were gradually suspending deliveries. Motorcycle orders could not be filled, product quality suffered, and revenues nosedived. Ducati was losing its Endgame branding/lifestyle niche because it was losing the product niche that supported it and the target-group niche that bought its products. It was ripe for a takeover, and the U.S. private-equity firm Texas Pacific Group (TPG) acquired Ducati. TPG recognized the value in Ducati's assets: talented engineers, leading engine technology, modern design, a strong fan club of motorcycle enthusiasts, and a racing team that had won numerous world titles. Ducati had potential; it just needed a turnaround strategy to capture it.

TPG initiated the Ducati turnaround by replacing the senior management team. Under the direction of new CEO Federico Minoli, the new management team developed a three-pronged turnaround strategy. First and foremost, the brand had to be revived to recapture and grow the customer base. The remaining two prongs of the strategy were to modernize production processes and improve motorcycle design.

The Ducati brand is built on its distinct characteristics—the desmodromic valve control, which produces a unique sound not replicated by any other motorcycle brand; the two-cylinder, L-shaped engine; the tube-frame construction; and, of course, the eye-catching Italian design.

To anchor and sustain its new marketing strategy, Ducati first had to reinforce its loyal fan base. The goal was to build bonds among Ducati owners through the shared lifestyle/experience of motorcycling, and to leverage those bonds to further the brand and ancillary sales—much as Harley-Davidson had done with its owners' group (H.O.G.) a decade earlier. Minoli said it best: "We are not about motorcycles, we are about motorcycling. My plan is to take Ducati from metal mechanics to entertainment, from motorcycles to motorcycling."

In 1997, Ducati started its first worldwide marketing campaign under the name "Ducatisti" (Ducati people). Ducatisti, as owners referred to themselves, were more than motorcycle riders; they were fans. Ducati then expanded its product portfolio to include clothing accessories and was the first motorcycle manufacturer to sell its products on the Internet.

To strengthen its brand image, Ducati opened its own flagship stores, the first one in New York City, with employees who are experienced motorcycle experts (rather than salespeople) that sell both motorcycles and apparel. TPG also built support for the Ducati brand with a product placement in the blockbuster movie *The Matrix Reloaded*.

As another component of its marketing strategy, Ducati streamlined the sales channel and created a tiered dealership structure with a focus that was more on selling quality and exclusivity than on quantity. The strategy paid off. Motorcycle sales rose by more than 30 percent annually from 1995 to 2003, even though the number of dealers was cut in half during the same period.

The turnaround also helped to modernize production. In 1997, Ducati implemented a just-in-time manufacturing philosophy, which, by 2003, resulted in faster production times (motorcycles were built in 10 hours rather than seven days) and a 50 percent increase in production (from 145 to 220 motorbikes per day). Collaborative relationships with key suppliers contributed to this new efficiency, as Ducati's suppliers negotiated with subcontractors on the company's behalf and Ducati went from having 420 vendors to 185.

Product development flourished following the takeover. Prior to 1996, Ducati's last major investment in engine development had been in 1988. In contrast, from 1996 to 2003, Ducati invested heavily in design and sped up product development; the time from idea to final product was reduced to 18 months, versus 36 months prior to the takeover. The new models introduced during this period included the popular 999 and the Multistrada.

The Ducati turnaround was celebrated by Ducati and its fans. From all corners of the world, more than 10,000 Ducatisti came to the first World Ducati Weekend near Bologna, Italy, in 1998. The World Ducati Week is now a four-day, annual event; in 2007, more than 25,000 Ducatisti roared into Bologna. With striking creativity, the company furthered its marketing activities with the opening of the Ducati Museum that celebrates the company's history and launching Ducati Racing to embrace motorsports and maintain the enthusiasm of the Ducati fan club.

In 1999, Ducati went public. From 1996 to 2003, the company's earnings before interest and taxes (EBIT) grew by approximately 20 percent annually, and Ducati's market share doubled. However, the 2004–2006 period saw declining revenues and losses, which Ducati and analysts attribute to aging designs and a soft market for Italian motorcycles. Thanks to a capital infusion to bolster motorcycle design, however, Ducati and the analysts expect the company to regain profitability by 2008.

After facing imminent bankruptcy, Ducati was able to stabilize its Endgame branding/lifestyle niche strategy by shoring up its product and target-group position. Its prospects for the future are brighter this time around, as Ducati is effectively managing its bundle of stable Endgame niche strategies.

Case Study 10

RED BULL: HOW A PRODUCT/BRANDING NICHE CHARGES AHEAD

Red Bull, the maker of a caffeinated energy drink, holds a stable Endgame niche in the beverage industry. Red Bull focuses on a single innovative product, using aggressive marketing tactics to propel it into a stable Endgame branding/lifestyle niche with cult status. Through Red Bull's success in marketing and product positioning, its product has been credited with creating a niche within a niche in which it has an undisputed monopoly. Red Bull has not only dominated but also defined the energy drink sector.

Red Bull owes its reinvigorating effects—and performance-enhancing capacity—to its main contents: caffeine, B vitamins, sugar, and taurine. It entered the Austrian market in 1987, based on a recipe from Thailand. The drink received mixed reviews from consumers who were not familiar with its sweet, highly carbonated taste. They couldn't understand its differentiation in the rapidly expanding ready-to-drink beverage sector. Clearly, the product was unique, but this was not sufficient to establish a stable Endgame product niche.

Red Bull's innovative marketing strategies are the linchpin of its success. Unlike competing brands, which spend between 10 and 15 percent of revenues on marketing efforts, Red Bull spends up to 40 percent of its revenues on marketing. Red Bull has always focused on the 18- to 30-year-old consumer segment and has never deliberately targeted jocks or athletic types. Instead, it has played up its hip factor and attracted students, young partygoers, and corporate newbies alike. With the slogan "Red Bull stimulates mind and body," the product claims to not only increase physical performance but also raise concentration levels and intellectual capacity. As a result, each person who consumes Red Bull identifies with being cool, physically fit, and smart, in addition to getting a shuddering jolt of caffeine and sugar. As part of this strategy, Red Bull uses viral marketing and word of mouth to build up its exclusivity factor.

To bring its product to market, the company promoted Red Bull at major local events in every country in which it is sold, and it achieved an edgy persona when the company sponsored extreme sports such as Formula One racing. In this way, Red Bull created its own target-group niche, attracting specific consumers and generating more demand. In April 2006, Red Bull was certified by the National Sports Foundation under the International Athletic Banned Substance Abuse Program. As the first energy drink to receive this certification, Red Bull reinforced its brand's association with extreme sports and invaded the sports drink market.

Red Bull also took a novel approach to distribution. Initially, the company shunned large-scale supermarkets and distributed Red Bull only in specialty stores. The drinks were delivered in striking silver-and-blue vehicles with a red bull on the hood that were unmistakably integrated into the brand. As demand for Red Bull rose and sales stabilized, the company relaxed its goal of building exclusivity. Today, Red Bull has a well-developed network of local subsidiaries that oversee dis-tribution for a given region. These subsidiaries are responsi-ble not only for importing the product from its sole point of production, but also for developing local marketing content, buzz marketing, and media buying (billboards, television, and so on). And despite calls for change, a single point of production has remained a successful distribution model for this increasingly stable Endgame product and target-group niche fighter.

The company has been able to maintain a firm grasp on its ever-exploding market. Energy drinks enjoyed a 12 percent compound annual growth rate (CAGR) during 2001–2005. While this figure is expected to decline to 9 percent for the years 2005–2010, it is still more than double the predicted CAGR for the soft drinks industry in general. Red Bull has maintained a commanding lead in the global energy drinks segment, capturing 28 percent of off-trade volume sales in 2005. PepsiCo and the Coca-Cola Company trailed behind, each with less than 10 percent of sales. In the United Kingdom, Red Bull accounts for 74 percent of off-premises volume sales and an increasing share of the on-premises market, in which Red Bull is a popular cocktail mixer. In the United States, Red Bull holds a sizable lead, with a 26 percent share of the total energy drinks market. Its closest competitor, PepsiCo's SoBe drink, has a 17 percent market share.

Currently, the small silver-and-blue cans with the bright Red Bull can be found in 130 countries. In 2006, 3 billion cans were sold worldwide, reaching $3.8 billion in sales. Red Bull is charging ahead with a stable Endgame niche strategy based on product, target-group, and branding/lifestyle niches.

Case Study 11

APPLE: FROM PRODUCT/BRANDING NICHE TO INNOVATION + COUNTER NICHE = SURPRISES ALL AROUND

Apple is a long-standing example of a stable Endgame product/branding niche. In the 1980s and 1990s, the Apple name and brand were synonymous with attractive design. However, its applications did not cater to the mass market; in the closing years of the last century, a smaller and smaller target group held the Apple brand in high esteem. Apple has since applied a dramatic concept and a couple of astounding innovative strategies that have transformed the company and the global consolidators it fights. The iPod and the iPhone are nothing short of textbook examples of stable Endgame innovation strategies.

With the iPod's arrival in 2001, Apple had introduced a revolutionary product in portable music devices. MP3 players had been on the market for a few years—they were just entering the Endgame Opening Phase—but none of the competing devices was compact, had much storage capacity, or was very user-friendly. From a design point of view, other MP3 players were mostly ugly little black and gray things that had more in common with the telephones of that era. More than just being the best in the small sector of MP3 players, the iPod effectively countered the global consolidators in the much larger—and much more consolidated—sector of portable media players. These consolidators, including Sony, knew a thing or two about giving people what they want.

Apple used its technical and design know-how in media storage and Internet-based service models to respond to the playback hardware guys, who were still busy thinking about how to make the Walkman smaller and smaller. While Sony was constrained by the size of the cassette, Apple asked the logical question: "What if the medium were invisible and infinitely small?"

In its first three years, Apple sold more than six million iPods. The legendary Sony Walkman needed twice that time to achieve the same level of sales in the early 1980s. In 2006 alone, Apple shipped more than 46 million iPods globally, and by the end of that year it held 72 percent of the U.S. market for MP3 players.

Because of the iPod's positive impact on the Apple brand, demand for Apple desktops and laptops also increased. Consequently, Apple's adjusted share price shot up 600 percent between the beginning of 2002 and the end of 2006. The iPod is now both a media device and a fashion statement, and is regarded worldwide as a hip accessory.

And the iPod product family is growing. Apple now offers iPods with multiple storage capacities and prices, including the iPod classic, shuffle, nano, and touch (an iPod with the look and feel of an iPhone). Extensive digital photo collections can be saved in the offerings with larger storage capacity. The nano and the shuffle are also available in association with the (PRODUCT) RED organization, with a portion of the proceeds being donated to fight AIDS in Africa.

Accessories for iPods expanded rapidly. These include trendy protective cases and wallets in a wide range of colors and materials. Speakers and portable devices for home use and adapters for automobile use are also available. You can even buy a transponder that slips into Nike+ running shoes and will transmit your heart rate to an iPod nano as it pumps Radiohead into your brain.

The iPod spawned the development of iTunes, an online application that allows customers to select and download MP3 files. As a result, online music piracy has been substantially reduced, as one can now download one's favorite songs legally and with ease in a "branded" environment. The comfort and ease of iTunes resulted in highly satisfied customers and a further strengthening of Apple's brand.

In 2007, Apple built on the success of the iPod by releasing the iPhone, a user-friendly media and communications device. With the iPhone, Apple effectively launched another innovation niche against the highly consolidated mobile telephone sector by adding Web-based and network technology to an elegant handset with an attractive graphical user interface. Customers stood in line for hours at Apple stores on launch day to buy the product. The iPhone, which runs on AT&T's global network, includes a touch-screen interface, Wi-Fi capability, a full-screen Web browser, a two-megapixel camera, an MP3 (the iPod!) player, and a video player. (The product can also serve as a phone!) Why didn't Nokia or Motorola come up with this idea three years earlier? Because they were in a late Endgame Focus phase battle of their own. Apple could not have timed its innovation niche strategy more perfectly.

A key component of the iPhone's successful launch was its pricing strategy, which reinforced Apple's innovation niche strategy. The iPhone was not a mobile handset, it was a way of life. During the summer 2007 launch, the iPhone started at $499, a comfortable $250 higher than the price point of the most expensive iPod—and with a flash drive that offered substantially less on-board memory. By doing this, Apple hoped to minimize iPod cannibalization by targeting a higher-end customer with even less price sensitivity than the iPod customer. Near the time of the launch, a customer survey revealed that price would be the most important factor in determining whether to purchase an iPhone. Apple subsequently lowered the price of the iPhone by $100, and even offered a rebate to customers who had paid the initial higher price. Following the launch, there was no clear evidence of iPod cannibalization. And in the first four months after the iPhone hit the store shelves, Apple's stock price increased by more than 50 percent.

Apple has since partnered with Starbucks to grow business in its current niche. As of fall 2007, iPods, iPhones, and iMac laptops in select Starbucks locations are now able to automatically detect and connect to iTunes without any Internet connection fee. In addition, the song currently playing inside each Starbucks will automatically appear on the device's screen, allowing the customer to download it immediately.

Apple has effectively stabilized its position against almost any global consolidator in the sectors in which it plays through a sophisticated bundle of stable Endgame product, target-group, and branding/lifestyle niche strategies, combined with stable Endgame innovation and counter niche approaches.

Case Study 12

RHÖN-KLINIKUM: LIGHTNING CONSOLIDATION CURES SICK HOSPITALS

More than 30 years ago, businessman Eugen Münch owned four brand-new 14-story buildings in the Franconia region in central Germany. In financial trouble and facing bankruptcy, Münch was looking for a new use for these buildings. He decided to establish a privately owned group of medical clinics, which soon evolved into a successful corporate group. Today, RHÖN-KLINIKUM AG is well known for hospital turnarounds and continues to acquire "ailing" hospitals. The RHÖN-KLINIKUM Group employs 31,000 professionals in 46 hospitals across Germany. In 2006, its profits were $153 million on sales of more than $2.8 billion.

The German hospital system is suffering from major financial, political, and demographic problems. Roughly 90 percent of German hospitals are run by government and nonprofit institutions and lag behind those in other developed nations in key areas. The rising costs of managing hospitals, coupled with increasing costs primarily from the state-funded health insurance system, are beginning to strain the system. At the same time, local governments and churches are withdrawing financing for hospitals because they do not have the necessary funds.

Politics and shifting demographics are also pressuring German hospitals. The government's recent enactment of health-care reforms places additional pressure on hospital administrators, as medical services are more strictly regulated.

Shifting demographics in Germany will add to the difficulty as medical needs rise along with the average age of the population.

As a result, the German hospital market is consolidating. Only major hospital groups are able to achieve economies of scale; they generally have higher utilization rates and therefore incur lower costs per patient visit. The consolidation trend is intersecting with another recent trend in German hospitals—privatization. Private hospitals are more flexible, are managed more effectively, and are more cost-conscious than their public counterparts. While today only 10 percent of hospitals are private, this number is expected to rise and to continue to rise well into the future.

Despite the challenges, RHÖN-KLINIKUM has been able to expand and prosper. It buys six to eight hospitals per year (a growth rate of approximately 800 beds per year) and follows a consistent strategy to integrate the hospitals effectively. Integration requires significant process transformations and personnel training. Indeed, the bottleneck in successful hospital acquisitions is not the availability of capital; it is the availability of professional management teams that are capable of integrating the newly acquired institutions. Eugen Münch and his team are experts in the takeover and reorganization of unprofitable hospitals, which consists primarily in reducing costs through improved processes while increasing the utilization of resources. Across all hospitals in the group, the average cost per bed is up to one-third lower than that in other private hospitals.

Once the RHÖN-KLINIKUM Group acquires an unprofitable hospital, it invests in technology and infrastructure to improve the hospital's processes, while also reducing personnel costs. Personnel costs are reduced by centralizing specific functions. For example, group hospitals use a "uniform treatment model" to place patients within the hospital. For patients who don't require frequent monitoring but are still admitted as inpatients, these hospitals provide low-care stations. Seriously ill patients who require more costly treatments and frequent monitoring are concentrated in intensive-care stations. This way, the number of personnel required is reduced. Each hospital makes its own personnel allocation decisions. Increasingly, RHÖN-KLINIKUM hospitals are moving patients to more cost-effective outpatient services, just as hospitals in the United States are doing. In Germany, only 5 to10 percent of acute-care patients are treated through outpatient services, compared to 60 percent in the United States.

In the next 10 years, the RHÖN-KLINIKUM Group plans to expand from 46 to 180 hospitals, which fits well with its goal of increasing market share from 3 percent to 10 percent—a sound goal for a stable Endgame niche. The strained German health-care system and limited public finances have created an excellent opportunity for a lightning consolidator such as the RHÖN-KLINIKUM Group.

Case Study 13

MITTAL STEEL: THE QUINTESSENTIAL LIGHTNING CONSOLIDATOR MELTS THE STEEL SECTOR

Through a series of shrewd takeovers, including acquiring U.S.-based International Steel Group (ISG) in 2005, Mittal Steel Company surpassed the former market leaders and reached the top of the global steel industry. In a market characterized by structural crisis, Mittal managed to recognize and exploit opportunities for strategic change. The firm accomplished this by developing a stellar in-house management team and by focusing its restructuring efforts on unprofitable steel companies, usually owned by former conglomerates. Because of the lightning-quick acquisition of market share, this scenario became known as "lightning consolidation."

After years of being in chronic crisis, the world market for raw steel recovered in 2004, primarily because of rising demand in the Asian market and a subsequent rise in prices. The steel industry today is clearly in the Scale Phase of consolidation. This phase is far from over. Indeed, it is more likely at its beginning.

Lakshmi Mittal was smart. He recognized global trends in the steel industry sooner than his competitors. He had gained firsthand experience in the industry as a 19-year-old trainee at his father's steel company in India, and expanded on this experience when at 26 he took over the management of a steelworks company in mostly unregulated Indonesia. It was clear to Mittal that rapid expansion was necessary for survival, so he concentrated on purchasing and reorganizing under-performing steel companies. He targeted existing companies rather than building new ones because it was significantly cheaper and quicker to do so. Before long, Lakshmi Mittal was dubbed a turnaround genius and was buying up companies in Eastern Europe and Central and North America.

Indeed, this lightning-consolidation strategy has made Lakshmi Mittal the trendsetter of global consolidation. After the takeover of ISG in April 2005, Mittal's U.S. operations generated more than $1.5 billion in operating income in 2006.

An important element of Mittal's success is the expertise of his management team. After each takeover, Mittal's team moves quickly to improve local management skills, optimize processes, and increase asset utilization at each plant. The basis for the team's success is not only its combined, specialized knowledge based on decades of experience, but also its ability to view each acquisition in the context of the global steel industry.

In addition, the company's global reach enables it to respond immediately to changes in both the market and production. For instance, recognizing the dangers of relying on a concentrated supplier market for raw materials, the steel giant reduced its raw material purchasing costs by 30 percent and capitalized on its vertical integration. Mittal made sure that the company was able to manage its requirements for iron ore and coking coal internally, with 40 and 100 percent, respectively.

Mittal Steel is continuing its ambitious agenda by targeting the vast Chinese market. In January 2005, Mittal Steel secured a 37 percent holding in Hunan Valin Steel Tube &

Wire, the eighth largest Chinese steel company. This was the first time a foreign company had purchased a large stake in a Chinese steel manufacturer. Mittal thereby gained major ground in the largest steel market in the world.

Mittal's most ambitious transaction to date is its 2006 merger with Luxembourg-based Arcelor. Initially, the company's bid for Arcelor, which would result in a 10 percent share of global steel production, was derided as unreasonably low. Lakshmi Mittal was not deterred; instead, he spent several months courting European investors and increasing the cash terms of the agreement. As a major concession, Mittal limited its stake in the merged firm to just 43.5 percent.

The Arcelor deal was different from other Mittal deals. First, Mittal did not receive a controlling stake in the new firm. And unlike previous purchases, in which Mittal acquired companies that were often unsuccessful or minor players in need of management know-how, Arcelor was a profitable giant in its own right. In 2005, Arcelor posted $4.8 billion in sales. As a result, it is unlikely to respond to changes by new management, and the existing Arcelor structure and operating system are likely to remain in place. This, of course, will make it difficult for Mittal to deliver on the promised $1.6 billion in synergies.

While Mittal's successful acquisition strategy and knowledgeable management team have built the largest steelmaker in the world, only time will tell whether its newest acquisition will create the path to the future that Lakshmi Mittal hopes for.

Case Study 14

KPMG: INTELLIGENT USE OF THE COOPERATION NICHE

It's hard to find a stable Endgame cooperation niche, but KPMG has managed to stake its claim in the financial auditing sector with an innovative, stable Endgame cooperation niche. Today, the global market for auditing is a hotly disputed oligopoly. The Big Four, which have emerged as the winners of the consolidation wave affecting the former Big Eight, provide auditing services for more than 78 percent of all U.S. joint stock companies and 99 percent of U.S. sales as of 2003.* One of the Big Four is KPMG, which reached sales of almost $17 billion in 2006. With approximately 113,000 employees in 148 countries and a leading position in several international markets, KPMG is among the largest audit and consultancy companies in the world.

KPMG is characterized by an extensive international reach and a decentralized structure. The company is made up of three worldwide divisions: audit, tax, and advisory. Since fall 2003, KPMG International has been structured as a "cooperative" under Swiss law. (KPMG International was previously organized as a group, with members creating national partnerships.) This structure—the cooperative niche—forms the basis of KPMG's enormous success.

KPMG does well in its regional markets, as member branches are able to develop rapidly and independently of any

---

*Data are from the U.S. Government Accountability Office. In addition to KPMG, the others in the Big Four are PricewaterhouseCoopers, Ernst & Young, and Deloitte & Touche.

central organization. Even though KPMG is represented externally in a uniform manner worldwide, the 93 national partnerships are independent legal structures. Separate ownership creates autonomy and means that liability risk is not shared around the network. KPMG International acts as an umbrella organization for the independent regional members. Other cooperatives have profited from this type of structure for decades—one example is the International Federation of Association Football (FIFA), which is also registered as an association in Switzerland and has 208 member associations.

Despite the strategic and financial success of KPMG's cooperation niche strategy, change may be on the horizon. Because of the perceived risk of accounting irregularities, there are increasing calls for uniform auditing standards, which means that national regulations could require regional or extraregional coordination. According to KPMG chairman Sir Michael Rake, if these developments continue, KPMG might need to better integrate its national companies into a more cohesively managed global group. Recent tax-fraud suits, in which some U.S. members were accused of setting up abusive tax shelters for clients, could pressure KPMG to increase its centralization and global standardization. If this happens, it could also undermine KPMG's cooperation niche strategy as a stable Endgame niche.

Case Study 15

SABRE: MARKET SPLITTER TAKES FLIGHT

It is only natural that the air travel industry would produce a stable Endgame market-splitting niche fighter, but it was a surprise that this would start so early and last so long. The core offering of U.S.-based Sabre Holdings is automated travel reservations through a travel global delivery system (GDS). Originally developed for American Airlines almost 50 years ago, Sabre was a proprietary, leading-edge software tool that was used to manage the airline's travel reservations system. By 2000, Sabre Holdings became independent when the division was spun off from American Airlines' parent company, AMR. In 2007, Sabre Holdings was purchased by the private-equity firm Texas Pacific Group in a deal valued at more than $5 billion.

The key to Sabre's success has been the transfer of critical resources to new products and markets and the permanent identification of new, high-revenue niches. Sabre has been able to build on its core competencies to establish and expand the entire GDS market by identifying new uses and channels. What was originally a proprietary software tool has become the backbone for flight, rail, hotel, rental car, and vacation cruise reservations that is used by travel providers, travel agents, and consumers. In 2004, Sabre was the largest GDS in the world, with a global market share of 36 percent. Its revenues grew from $2.1 billion in 2004 to $2.8 billion in 2006. Many consumers will be familiar with Sabre's best-known brand, Travelocity, a leader in the global online travel reservations market.

The idea of setting up a database to manage airline seat reservations came to two senior managers of American Airlines and IBM, who sat together on a flight from Los Angeles to New York in 1953. (1953 was the last year in which more passengers traveled across the Atlantic by ocean steamer than by airplane, which reinforces the dramatic role that technology plays in our industrial development.) Although it took seven years for the two companies to develop SABRE (Semi-Automated Business Research Environment), when the system was completed in 1960, it revolutionized the aviation industry.

In 1976, SABRE was extended to travel agencies so that they could assist their clients in booking flights on American Airlines. In 1986, SABRE was renamed Sabre (with only the S capitalized) and became an independent subsidiary of AMR. Also in the 1980s, the Sabre network was extended to airlines in Canada and the United Kingdom, paving the way for further international expansion. Faced with competition from similar global delivery systems developed by other airlines and rapid industry consolidation, Sabre maintained its market share by continuing to be first to market in each new delivery channel. It also remained the cost leader in reservation systems. Entering the 1990s, Sabre saw little opportunity left in the original flight reservations niche as a result of industry consolidation and vigorously sought new customers and markets that could be served with Sabre's technology.

Today, Sabre consists of three main business divisions that are separated by distribution channel, with each division offering multiple brands. Sabre Airlines Solutions continues to operate in its original niche and provides leading-edge software and services to airlines and other providers. Sabre Travel Network leverages the Sabre reservations system to sell flights, hotel reservations, car rentals, cruises, and tour packages through travel agencies. Travelocity is Sabre's own online travel agency, which sells travel products directly to consumers.

Sabre has remained a market leader in a highly competitive environment. The company is likely to maintain its status through constant innovation and finding new market applications for its core technology. It has developed a modular business model that enables it to transfer its core technology to new market applications rapidly and inexpensively. In this way, Sabre is securing a speed and cost advantage in new business areas that cannot be matched by many other companies.

Despite its large number of brands and acquisitions, Sabre has maintained continuity in how it applies its core competency to new markets. Executives recognized early on that its key competency was not the simple reservations system, but the ability to book trips efficiently. Sabre did not believe in the boundaries of its original market niche. By employing a broad interpretation of its vision and mission, Sabre was able to recognize the full potential of the travel reservations industry. Its success is a result of the development of market-ready products and continuing to split the market by placing these products in newly created channels and subniches.

Sabre serves all customers in the travel reservations market through 12 key brands. A sampling of these brands includes SynXis to serve hotel suppliers, Nexion to serve travel agencies, and Travelocity and lastminute.com to bring self-service travel reservations to the consumer. Each brand is based on the same core competency or is connected with Sabre GDS in an integrated way. Through these brands, Sabre plans to remain the market leader and continue to be synonymous with the travel reservations industry.

Appendix A

About the Stable Endgame Niche Strategies Study

The Value Building Growth study (published in 2000 under the title *The Growth Code Deciphered*[*]) is a comprehensive database of worldwide corporate economic activity that has been expanded over the years. It comprises approximately 32,000 publicly traded companies and an additional 630,000 privately held companies. This database contains highly relevant information, particularly for public companies, but we have also made a consistent and continuous effort to flesh out a clear understanding of how privately held companies operate. Although there are noticeable holes in the data on privately held companies, we believe that the Value Building Growth study represents the world's most complete representation of global corporate activity in existence today, with well over 98 percent of global activity included.

This database has enabled us to understand why certain companies outperform others in their industry in both sales growth and value (market capitalization) growth. The empirical data of the Value Building Growth study allow us to locate each industry player within a quadrant that reflects not only its success in the marketplace, but also its valuation by the capital markets. Figure A-1 is a schematic of the Value Building Growth matrix, with summary data.

---

[*]Fritz Kroeger, Michael Träm, Jörg Rockenhäuser, James McGrath, *The Growth Code Deciphered: Strategies for Increasing the Value of Companies* (Wiesbaden, 2000).

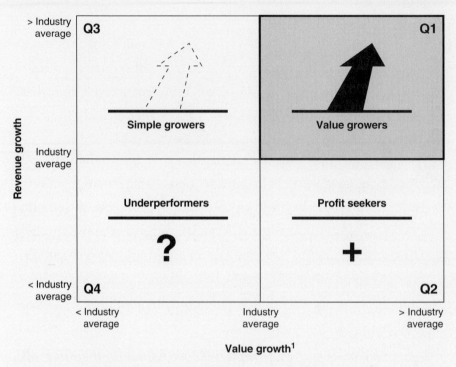

Figure A-1 Value Building Growth matrix

This database was also used to derive the Merger Endgame Theory (published in 2000 under the title *Merger Endgames: Strategies for the Consolidation Wave*[†]), in which industry movement and overall consolidation trends were analyzed over time. In a more detailed analysis of the Endgame concept, we found that many so-called niche strategies were profoundly unstable over the life cycle of global industrial consolidation.

[†]Graeme Deans, Fritz Kroeger, and Stefan Zeisel, *Merger Endgames: Strategies for the Consolidation Wave* (Wiesbaden, 2002).

To further illuminate this phenomenon, we designed the Endgame niche study. We started with the understanding that there are successful small companies in every stage of industry consolidation—even in the later phases of the Endgame curve—and that our empirical data proved Michael Porter's theoretical U curve. However, we also found that these smaller "high-performing companies" became increasingly rare in each successive Endgame phase, as each industry sector consolidated.

From the 32,000 public companies and the maximum number of available private companies for which we could derive information, we identified those companies that had achieved the highest revenue growth and highest market capitalization growth over a sustained period of time. Thus, we had 600 stable Endgame niche fighters worldwide.

For each of the 600 companies, we brought together all the information that was available in databases worldwide and compared it with the information in our Value Building Growth database. We then analyzed these companies further using all externally available qualitative information, including mission statements, company reports over a 10-year period, Web sites, and other publications.

Using this information, we analyzed the stated corporate strategy of each company over time, its geographic expansion, and other elements of organic and nonorganic growth. This analysis was used to determine which strategies allowed these niche fighters to maintain their performance—and their existence—over an extended period of time. Our conclusions were again evaluated against the Value Building Growth database. The industries in which the companies operated were reviewed in the context of the

Merger Endgame life-cycle curve (divided into 16 subphases), which produced the Endgame niche graphic with the industries identified.

Throughout the two-year study, the findings were tested for relevance and stability, both within the A.T. Kearney network and with interested client companies.

Appendix B | Distribution of Stable Endgame Niches— Summary

Main Industries	Number of Companies	Regional	Target-Group	Branding/Lifestyle	Product	Speed/Lightning-Consolidation	Innovation	Cooperation	Market-Splitting	Counter
Aluminum, Steel, Construction	13	15%	0%	0%	39%	77%	0%	8%	15%	0%
Automotive OEMs, Automotive Suppliers, Rubber and Tire Producers	15	0%	0%	7%	100%	67%	87%	27%	13%	0%
Banks, Insurance	7	71%	14%	0%	86%	29%	0%	43%	14%	14%
Energy, Oil, Gas	13	46%	0%	0%	62%	54%	15%	8%	8%	0%
Food, Beverages, Dairy, Cigarettes	53	26%	0%	36%	51%	72%	21%	19%	2%	2%
Hotels	5	40%	20%	20%	60%	40%	0%	0%	0%	0%
Mechanical Engineering, Chemicals, High Tech, Pharma	96	0%	0%	2%	95%	57%	66%	13%	9%	2%
Retail, Restaurants and Fast Food	34	71%	24%	18%	59%	47%	15%	3%	0%	3%
Services	17	59%	0%	0%	35%	65%	6%	6%	12%	0%
Telecom, Transport	17	35%	0%	0%	65%	65%	12%	12%	0%	0%
Total*	270	26%	4%	11%	71%	60%	36%	13%	7%	2%

*Not an average, but a split set for the total

Sources: Value Building Growth database; A.T. Kearney analysis

Appendix C

The 600 Stable Endgame Niche Fighters

Entity Name	Company Status	S-Curve (4 Phases)	S-Curve (16 Phases)	Industry	Country
A. Palliser SA	Non-listed	Scale	5	Wholesalers	Spain
Aalberts Industries N.V.	Listed	Focus	9	Metal Producers	Netherlands
Aaron Rents, Inc.	Listed	Scale	5	Department Stores	United States
ABC Supply Co. Inc.	Non-listed	Scale	5	Wholesalers	United States
Abertis Infraestructuras S.A.	Listed	Opening	3	Service Organisations	Spain
ACC Limited	Listed	Scale	6	Cement Producers	India
Ace Cash Express	Listed	Scale	8	Financial Services	United States
Acqua Minerale San Benedetto	Non-listed	Scale	6	Brewers	Italy
ACS Actividades Construccion Y Servicios	Listed	Opening	2	Construction	Spain
Adelaide Brighton Ltd.	Listed	Scale	6	Cement Producers	Australia
Adolf Würth GmbH & Co.	Non-listed	Scale	5	Wholesalers	Germany
Advanced Micro Devices, Inc.	Listed	Focus	9	Electronic Data Processing Equipment	Canada
AECOM	Non-listed	Opening	2	Construction	United States
Aegis Group plc	Listed	Focus	9	Advertising Agencies	United Kingdom
Agrana Beteiligungs, AG	Listed	Scale	7	Sugar Producers	Austria
Airgas, Inc.	Listed	Scale	5	Wholesalers	United States
Akbank TAS	Listed	Scale	5	Commercial Banks	Turkey
Alabama National Bancorporation	Listed	Scale	5	Commercial Banks	United States
Alamo Group Incorporated	Listed	Scale	7	Machinery	United States
Alba PLC	Listed	Focus	9	Appliances & Consumer Products	United Kingdom
Albany International	Listed	Scale	6	Textiles	United States
Albron B.V.	Non-listed	Scale	5	Restaurants & Fast Food Franchisers	Netherlands
ALCO Stores	Listed	Focus	11	Discount Stores	United States
Aleris International, Inc	Listed	Balance	13	Aluminum Producers	United States
Alexon Group PLC	Listed	Scale	5	Apparel Manufacturers	United Kingdom
Alimerka SA	Non-listed	Scale	5	Department Stores	Spain
Alliance Atlantis Communications Inc	Listed	Focus	11	Motion Picture Producers & Dists.	Canada
Alliance Unichem PLC	Listed	Scale	5	Wholesalers	United Kingdom
Alliant Tech System Inc.	Listed	Scale	6	Miscellaneous Aerospace	United States
Allied Electronics Inc.	Listed	Focus	9	Electronics	South Africa

Sources: Value Building Growth database; A. T. Kearney analysis

Appendix C. The 600 Stable Endgame Niche Fighters *(continued)*

Entity Name	Company Status	S-Curve (4 Phases)	S-Curve (16 Phases)	Industry	Country
Alma Media	Listed	Scale	6	Newspaper Publishers	Finland
Almacenes Electricos Vascongados SA	Non-listed	Scale	5	Wholesalers	Spain
Altis Semiconductor	Non-listed	Focus	9	Electronics	France
Ambac Assurance Corp.	Listed	Scale	5	Insurance Companies	United States
Ambuja Cements Limited	Listed	Scale	6	Cement Producers	India
America Service Group Inc.	Listed	Scale	6	Medical Services	United States
American Eagle Outfitters, Inc.	Listed	Scale	6	Apparel Store Chains	United States
America's Drive-In Brand Properties, Inc.	Listed	Scale	5	Restaurants & Fast Food Franchisers	United States
AmeriCredit Corp.	Listed	Scale	5	Commercial Banks	United States
Amorepacific	Listed	Scale	5	Cosmetics & Toiletries	Korea, Republic of
Anadolu Efes A.S.	Listed	Scale	6	Brewers	Turkey
Anglo Irish Bank Corporation, plc	Listed	Scale	5	Commercial Banks	Ireland
Ann Taylor Retail, Inc.	Listed	Scale	6	Apparel Store Chains	United States
Apetito AG	Non-listed	Scale	6	Food	Germany
APN News & Media	Listed	Scale	6	Newspaper Publishers	Australia
Apollo Group, Inc.	Listed	Opening	3	Service Organisations	United States
Applebee's IP LLC	Listed	Scale	5	Restaurants & Fast Food Franchisers	United States
Aqua America, Inc.	Listed	Scale	8	Water Companies	United States
Aqualia Gestion Integral del Agua S.A.	Non-listed	Scale	8	Water Companies	Spain
ARC Energy Trust	Listed	Focus	9	Oil & Gas	Canada
Arco Limited	Non-listed	Scale	5	Wholesalers	United Kingdom
Arctic Cat Inc.	Listed	Scale	5	Original Parts & Accessories Mfrs.	United States
Arneg S.p.A.	Non-listed	Scale	6	Furnishings	Italy
Ase Group	Listed	Focus	9	Electronic Data Processing Equipment	Taiwan, Province of China
Asia Optical Co., Inc.	Listed	Focus	11	Photographic Equipment & Supplies	Taiwan, Province of China
Asian Paints Ltd.	Listed	Scale	7	Paint & Resin Manufacturers	India
ASM International N.V.	Listed	Scale	7	Machinery	Netherlands
Asmo Co., Ltd	Non-listed	Focus	9	Electronics	Japan
Atel	Listed	Opening	2	Utilities	Switzerland
Atenor Group	Listed	Scale	5	Wholesalers	Belgium

Sources: Value Building Growth database; A.T. Kearney analysis

Appendix C. The 600 Stable Endgame Niche Fighters *(continued)*

Entity Name	Company Status	S-Curve (4 Phases)	S-Curve (16 Phases)	Industry	Country
Atlas Copco AB	Listed	Scale	7	Machinery	Sweden
Australia and New Zealand Banking Group Limited (ANZ)	Listed	Scale	5	Commercial Banks	Australia
B/E Aerospace, Inc.	Listed	Scale	6	Miscellaneous Aerospace	United States
BAE Systems	Listed	Focus	9	Scientific Equipment & Supplies	United States
Banca Popolare di Sondrio	Listed	Scale	5	Commercial Banks	Italy
Banco di Desio e della Brianza	Listed	Scale	5	Commercial Banks	Italy
Bandai Co., LTD.	Listed	Scale	7	Games & Toys	Japan
Bangchak Petroleum Public Company Limited, The	Listed	Focus	9	Oil & Gas	Thailand
Bank Of Queensland Limited ABN	Listed	Scale	5	Commercial Banks	Australia
Barnes Group Inc.	Listed	Focus	9	Wire, Chain & Spring	United States
Barr Pharmaceuticals, Inc.	Listed	Scale	5	Pharma, Drugs & Health Care	United States
Battelle Memorial Institute	Non-listed	Focus	9	Electronics	United States
Baytex Energy Trust	Listed	Focus	9	Oil & Gas	Canada
Bed Bath & Beyond Inc.	Listed	Scale	5	Department Stores	United States
Beijer Alma	Listed	Focus	9	Wire, Chain & Spring	Sweden
Belgacom	Non-listed	Opening	3	Service Organisations	Belgium
Bell AG	Listed	Focus	9	Meat Packers	Switzerland
Bendigo and Adelaide Bank Limited, ABN	Listed	Scale	5	Commercial Banks	Australia
Bettys & Taylors Group Ltd.	Non-listed	Scale	5	Restaurants & Fast Food Franchisers	United Kingdom
Beverage Brands	Non-listed	Scale	6	Brewers	United Kingdom
Beverage Japan, Inc.	Non-listed	Scale	5	Restaurants & Fast Food Franchisers	Japan
Bijou Brigitte modische Accessoires AG	Listed	Scale	5	Apparel Manufacturers	Germany
Biogen Idec	Listed	Scale	5	Pharma, Drugs & Health Care	United States
Biomet, Inc.	Listed	Scale	5	Medical, Surgical & Dental Suppliers	United States
Bluegreen Vacations Unlimited, Inc.	Listed	Opening	3	Real Estate	United States
Body Shop International, plc, The	Listed	Scale	5	Cosmetics & Toiletries	United Kingdom
Boiron Group	Listed	Scale	5	Pharma, Drugs & Health Care	France
Bongaigaon Refinery and Petrochemicals Limited	Listed	Focus	9	Oil & Gas	India
Boston Private Wealth Management Group	Listed	Scale	5	Commercial Banks	United States
Boston Scientific Corporation	Listed	Scale	5	Medical, Surgical & Dental Suppliers	United States

Sources: Value Building Growth database; A.T. Kearney analysis

Appendix C. The 600 Stable Endgame Niche Fighters *(continued)*

Entity Name	Company Status	S-Curve (4 Phases)	S-Curve (16 Phases)	Industry	Country
Bowe Systec AG	Listed	Focus	12	Business Machines & Office Equipment	Germany
Brickworks Limited	Listed	Scale	5	Brick, Clay & Refractory Products	Australia
BSS Group plc, The	Listed	Scale	5	Wholesalers	United Kingdom
Burberry Limited	Non-listed	Scale	5	Apparel Manufacturers	United Kingdom
C & W Berry Ltd	Non-listed	Scale	5	Wholesalers	United Kingdom
Calor	Non-listed	Focus	9	Electronics	France
Canadian Natural	Listed	Focus	9	Oil & Gas	Canada
Capital One Services, Inc.	Listed	Scale	8	Financial Services	United States
Carraro Group	Listed	Scale	7	Machinery	Italy
Cascades Inc.	Listed	Scale	5	Packaging Products	Canada
Cathay Bank	Listed	Scale	5	Commercial Banks	United States
Cattles PLC	Listed	Scale	5	Commercial Banks	United Kingdom
CBL & Associates Properties, Inc.	Listed	Opening	3	Real Estate	United States
CCT Telecom Holdings Limited	Listed	Focus	9	Electronics	Hong Kong
CDW Corporation	Listed	Scale	5	Wholesalers	United States
CEC Entertainment	Listed	Scale	5	Restaurants & Fast Food Franchisers	United States
Celesio Agency	Listed	Scale	5	Wholesalers	Germany
Celgene Corporation	Listed	Scale	5	Pharma, Drugs & Health Care	United States
Cementir S.p.A.	Non-listed	Scale	6	Cement Producers	Italy
CEMENTOS MOLINS S.A.	Non-listed	Scale	6	Cement Producers	Spain
Cementos Portland Valderrivas	Listed	Scale	6	Cement Producers	Spain
Cephalon, Inc.	Listed	Scale	5	Pharma, Drugs & Health Care	United States
CEPSA	Non-listed	Scale	5	Chemicals	Spain
Ceradyne, Inc.	Listed	Scale	5	Chemicals	United States
Cerypsa Ceramicas S.A.	Non-listed	Scale	5	Brick, Clay & Refractory Products	Spain
CET Electric S.R.L.	Non-listed	Scale	6	Industrial & Comm Elect. Equipment	Italy
Charming Shoppes, Inc.	Listed	Scale	6	Apparel Store Chains	United States
Cheesecake Factory Incorporated, The	Listed	Scale	5	Restaurants & Fast Food Franchisers	United States
Chesapeake Energy Corporation	Listed	Focus	9	Exploration, Drilling Service & Equipment	United States
Chico's Retail Services, Inc.	Listed	Scale	6	Apparel Store Chains	United States

Sources: Value Building Growth database; A.T. Kearney analysis

Appendix C. The 600 Stable Endgame Niche Fighters *(continued)*

Entity Name	Company Status	S-Curve (4 Phases)	S-Curve (16 Phases)	Industry	Country
Chugai Pharmaceutical Co. Ltd	Listed	Scale	5	Pharma, Drugs & Health Care	Japan
Chugoku Marine Paints, Ltd.	Listed	Scale	7	Paint & Resin Manufacturers	Japan
Chuo Gyorui, Co. Ltd.	Non-listed	Scale	5	Department Stores	Japan
Church & Dwight Co., Inc.	Listed	Scale	5	Chemicals	United States
CI Financial Income Fund	Listed	Scale	8	Financial Services	Canada
Cinram International Inc	Listed	Focus	9	Electronics	Canada
Citrix Systems, Inc.	Listed	Scale	8	Systems & Subsystems	United States
Clarins PARIS, LLC	Listed	Scale	5	Cosmetics & Toiletries	France
Clinton Cards	Listed	Scale	5	Department Stores	United Kingdom
CMC Magnetics Corporation	Listed	Focus	9	Electronics	Taiwan, Province of China
Cobham plc	Listed	Scale	6	Miscellaneous Aerospace	United Kingdom
Coca-Cola West Holdings Co. Ltd	Listed	Focus	9	Soft Drink Producers & Bottlers	Japan
Colas SA	Listed	Opening	2	Construction	France
Coloplast Group	Listed	Scale	5	Medical, Surgical & Dental Suppliers	Denmark
Commerce Bancorp, Inc.	Listed	Scale	5	Commercial Banks	United States
Community Bank, N.A.	Listed	Scale	5	Commercial Banks	United States
Computer Sciences Corporation	Listed	Focus	9	Electronics	United States
Comtech Telecommuications Corp.	Listed	Focus	12	Business Machines & Office Equipment	United States
Cooper Companies, Inc., The	Listed	Scale	5	Pharma, Drugs & Health Care	United States
Cooperativa Italiana di Ristorazione	Non-listed	Scale	6	Food	Italy
Cott Corporation	Listed	Focus	9	Soft Drink Producers & Bottlers	Canada
Couche-Tard Inc.	Listed	Scale	5	Department Stores	Canada
Cracker Barrel Old Country Store, Inc.	Listed	Scale	5	Restaurants & Fast Food Franchisers	United States
Cranswick Plc	Listed	Scale	6	Food	United Kingdom
Credit Saison Co., Ltd.	Listed	Scale	5	Commercial Banks	Japan
Cree, Inc.	Listed	Focus	9	Electronic Data Processing Equipment	United States
Cremonini S.p.A.	Non-listed	Scale	5	Restaurants & Fast Food Franchisers	Italy
Crerar Hotel Group	Non-listed	Scale	5	Hotel & Motel Chains	United Kingdom
Crescent Stoneco	Listed	Scale	6	Industrial & Comm Elect. Equipment	United States
CSL Limited	Listed	Scale	5	Pharma, Drugs & Health Care	Australia

Sources: Value Building Growth database; A. T. Kearney analysis

Appendix C. The 600 Stable Endgame Niche Fighters *(continued)*

Entity Name	Company Status	S-Curve (4 Phases)	S-Curve (16 Phases)	Industry	Country
Curtiss-Wright Corporation	Listed	Focus	11	Engines	United States
D.R. Horton, Inc.	Listed	Scale	5	Home Builders	United States
Daikin Europe N.V.	Non-listed	Scale	7	Machinery	Belgium
Daiko Electric Co., Ltd.	Non-listed	Scale	6	Electrical	Japan
Daishinseiki Co., Ltd.	Non-listed	Scale	5	Original Parts & Accessories Mfrs.	Japan
Daktronics, Inc.	Listed	Focus	12	Business Machines & Office Equipment	United States
Darden Concepts, Inc.	Listed	Scale	5	Restaurants & Fast Food Franchisers	United States
Davide Campari-Milano S.p.a.	Non-listed	Scale	6	Brewers	Italy
DCC plc	Listed	Focus	12	Business Machines & Office Equipment	Ireland
De Hoop Terneuzen BV	Non-listed	Scale	5	Wholesalers	Netherlands
Deceuninck NV	Listed	Scale	5	Chemicals	Belgium
Delphi Financial Group, Inc.	Listed	Scale	5	Insurance Companies	United States
Denbury Resources Inc.	Listed	Focus	9	Oil & Gas	Canada
Dendrite International	Listed	Focus	9	Electronics	United States
Denso Corporation	Non-listed	Focus	9	Electronics	Japan
Dentsply International	Listed	Scale	5	Medical, Surgical & Dental Suppliers	United States
Deutz AG	Listed	Scale	7	Machinery	Germany
Developers Diversified Realty	Listed	Opening	3	Real Estate	United States
Diesel S.p.A.	Non-listed	Scale	5	Apparel Manufacturers	Italy
Donaldson Company, Inc.	Listed	Scale	7	Machinery	United States
Dong-A Pharmaceutical	Listed	Scale	5	Pharma, Drugs & Health Care	Korea, Republic of
Dorel Industries, Inc.	Listed	Scale	6	Furnishings	Canada
Dorman Products	Listed	Scale	5	Wholesalers	United States
Dr. Reddy's Laboratories Ltd.	Listed	Scale	5	Pharma, Drugs & Health Care	India
Draegerwerk AG & Co.	Listed	Focus	9	Scientific Equipment & Supplies	Germany
Drew Industries Incorporated	Listed	Scale	5	Metal Products	United States
DRS Technologies, Inc.	Listed	Balance	15	Gov't & Defense Electronic Systems	United States
Duerr AG	Listed	Scale	7	Machinery	Germany
E.W. Scripps Company, The	Listed	Scale	6	Newspaper Publishers	United States
Ebro Puleva Grupo	Listed	Scale	7	Sugar Producers	Spain

Sources: Value Building Growth database; A.T. Kearney analysis

212

Appendix C. The 600 Stable Endgame Niche Fighters *(continued)*

Entity Name	Company Status	S-Curve (4 Phases)	S-Curve (16 Phases)	Industry	Country
Echostar Corporation	Listed	Scale	5	Radio & T.V. Broadcasts	United States
Ecolab Inc.	Listed	Scale	5	Chemicals	United States
Edcon	Listed	Scale	6	Apparel Store Chains	South Africa
Edward Jones	Non-listed	Scale	8	Financial Services	United States
Ekornes ASA	Listed	Scale	6	Furnishings	Norway
El Corte Ingles S.A.	Non-listed	Scale	5	Department Stores	Spain
Elizabeth Arden, Inc.	Listed	Scale	5	Cosmetics & Toiletries	United States
ElringKlinger AG	Listed	Scale	5	Original Parts & Accessories Mfrs.	Germany
Embraco	Listed	Scale	7	Machinery	Brazil
Emeritus Corporation	Listed	Opening	3	Service Organisations	United States
Empresas CMPC S.A.	Listed	Scale	5	Packaging Products	Chile
Ensign Services Inc	Listed	Focus	9	Exploration, Drilling Service & Equipment	Canada
Enterprise Inns plc.	Listed	Scale	6	Recreation	United Kingdom
Esprit Holdings Limited	Listed	Scale	6	Apparel Store Chains	Hong Kong
Essex Property Trust, Inc.	Listed	Opening	3	Real Estate	United States
Esterline Technologies Corporation	Listed	Focus	9	Electronics	United States
Eurokai Kgaa AG	Listed	Scale	8	Freight Forwarders	Germany
Expeditors International Of Washington, Inc.	Listed	Scale	8	Freight Forwarders	United States
F&C Investments	Listed	Scale	8	Financial Services	United Kingdom
F.Lli Lando	Non-listed	Scale	5	Department Stores	Italy
Fakta A/S	Non-listed	Scale	5	Department Stores	Denmark
Family Dollar Stores, Inc.	Listed	Scale	5	Department Stores	United States
Fastenal Company	Listed	Scale	5	Wholesalers	United States
FBD Holdings plc	Listed	Scale	5	Insurance Companies	Ireland
FEI Company	Listed	Scale	5	Original Parts & Accessories Mfrs.	United States
Festina Group	Non-listed	Scale	5	Wholesalers	Switzerland
Fiesta Hotels Group	Non-listed	Scale	5	Hotel & Motel Chains	Spain
Finish Line, Inc., The	Listed	Focus	9	Shoe Retailers	United States
FLIR Worldwide	Listed	Scale	5	Instruments, Gauges & Meters	United States
Fluchos SL	Non-listed	Focus	10	Shoe Manufacturers	Spain

Sources: Value Building Growth database; A.T. Kearney analysis

Appendix C. The 600 Stable Endgame Niche Fighters *(continued)*

Entity Name	Company Status	S-Curve (4 Phases)	S-Curve (16 Phases)	Industry	Country
Fomento Economico Mexicano S.A. de C.V.	Listed	Scale	6	Brewers	Mexico
Forest Laboratories, Inc.	Listed	Scale	5	Pharma, Drugs & Health Care	United States
Formosa Chemicals & Fibre Corporation	Listed	Scale	5	Chemicals	Taiwan, Province of China
Fosfertil SA	Listed	Scale	5	Chemicals	Brazil
Fossil, Inc.	Listed	Focus	9	Electronics	United States
Foxconn Electronics, Inc.	Listed	Focus	11	Photographic Equipment & Supplies	Taiwan, Province of China
Franklin Electric Co, Inc.	Listed	Scale	6	Industrial & Comm Elect. Equipment	United States
Fred's Inc.	Listed	Focus	11	Discount Stores	United States
French Connection	Listed	Scale	5	Apparel Manufacturers	United Kingdom
Fromageries Bel	Listed	Scale	6	Dairy Products	France
Fuchs Petrolub AG	Listed	Focus	9	Oil & Gas	Germany
Fujitsu Frontech Limited	Listed	Focus	9	Electronic Data Processing Equipment	Japan
Gabarro Hermanos S.A.	Non-listed	Scale	5	Wholesalers	Spain
Galenica Group, The	Listed	Scale	5	Wholesalers	Switzerland
Galliford Try	Listed	Opening	2	Construction	United Kingdom
Gardner Denver Thomas, Inc	Listed	Focus	9	Appliances & Consumer Products	United States
Gardner Denver, Inc.	Listed	Scale	7	Machinery	United States
Garmin Ltd.	Listed	Scale	5	Instruments, Gauges & Meters	United States
Gelsenwasser AG	Listed	Scale	8	Water Companies	Germany
General Growth Properties, Inc.	Listed	Opening	3	Real Estate	United States
Gentex Corporation	Listed	Scale	5	Original Parts & Accessories Mfrs.	United States
Genuine Parts Company	Listed	Scale	5	Wholesalers	United States
Genzyme Corporation	Listed	Scale	5	Pharma, Drugs & Health Care	United States
Getinge Group	Listed	Scale	5	Medical, Surgical & Dental Suppliers	Sweden
Gilead	Listed	Scale	5	Pharma, Drugs & Health Care	United States
Glanbia PLC	Listed	Scale	6	Dairy Products	Ireland
Go-Ahead Group plc., The	Listed	Scale	8	Freight Forwarders	United Kingdom
Graco Inc	Listed	Scale	7	Machinery	United States
Grafton Group plc	Listed	Scale	5	Wholesalers	Ireland
Greencore Group	Listed	Scale	6	Food	Ireland

Sources: Value Building Growth database; A.T. Kearney analysis

Appendix C. The 600 Stable Endgame Niche Fighters *(continued)*

Entity Name	Company Status	S-Curve (4 Phases)	S-Curve (16 Phases)	Industry	Country
Greene King Brewing and Retailing Limited	Listed	Scale	6	Brewers	United Kingdom
Greggs plc	Listed	Focus	11	Bakers	United Kingdom
Groupe Beneteau	Listed	Focus	9	Shipbuilding	France
Grupa Zywiec S.A.	Listed	Scale	6	Brewers	Poland
Grupo Bimbo SAB de CV	Listed	Scale	6	Food	Mexico
Grupo Elektra, SA de CV	Listed	Scale	5	Department Stores	Mexico
Grupo FCC	Listed	Opening	2	Construction	Spain
Grupo Salvador Caetano	Listed	Scale	7	Automotive Manufacturers	Portugal
Grupo Suzano	Listed	Scale	5	Paper	Brazil
Grupos Norte SA	Non-listed	Scale	5	Wholesalers	Spain
Guyenne et Gascogne	Listed	Scale	6	Food	France
Halcon Ceramicas, S.A.	Non-listed	Scale	5	Brick, Clay & Refractory Products	Spain
Haldex	Listed	Scale	5	Original Parts & Accessories Mfrs.	Sweden
Halma p.l.c.	Listed	Scale	7	Machinery	United Kingdom
HanGlas	Listed	Focus	9	Glass	Korea, Republic of
Hankook Tire	Listed	Focus	9	Rubber & Tire Mfrs.	Korea, Republic of
Hans Einhell AG	Listed	Scale	7	Machinery	Germany
Hansol Paper	Listed	Scale	6	Printing & Writing Paper	Korea, Republic of
Harris Corporation	Listed	Focus	9	Electronics	United States
HCC Insurance Holdings, Inc.	Listed	Scale	5	Insurance Companies	United States
Headlam Group plc	Listed	Scale	5	Wholesalers	United Kingdom
Heartland Express Inc.	Listed	Scale	5	Trucking	United States
Heiwa Corporation	Listed	Scale	7	Games & Toys	Japan
Hexagon	Listed	Scale	5	Instruments, Gauges & Meters	Sweden
Hilton Hospitality, Inc.	Listed	Scale	5	Hotel & Motel Chains	United States
Hite Brewery Company Limited	Listed	Scale	6	Brewers	Korea, Republic of
Holly Corporation	Listed	Focus	9	Oil & Gas	United States
Homeserve	Listed	Focus	9	Electronics	United Kingdom
Hon Hai Precision Industries Company	Listed	Focus	9	Electronic Data Processing Equipment	Taiwan, Province of China
Honam Petrochemicals Corp.	Listed	Scale	7	Paint & Resin Manufacturers	Korea, Republic of

Sources: Value Building Growth database; A.T. Kearney analysis

Appendix C. The 600 Stable Endgame Niche Fighters *(continued)*

Entity Name	Company Status	S-Curve (4 Phases)	S-Curve (16 Phases)	Industry	Country
Horiba, Ltd.	Listed	Scale	5	Instruments, Gauges & Meters	Japan
Horie Metal Co., Ltd.	Non-listed	Scale	5	Metal Products	Japan
Hospitality Properties Trust	Listed	Opening	3	Real Estate	United States
Housing Development Finance Corporation Limited	Listed	Scale	5	Commercial Banks	India
HTL International Holdings Ltd.	Listed	Scale	6	Furnishings	Singapore
Hubbell Incorporated	Listed	Scale	6	Industrial & Comm Elect. Equipment	United States
Huntleigh Technology PLC	Listed	Scale	5	Medical, Surgical & Dental Suppliers	United Kingdom
Hymer AG	Listed	Scale	7	Automotive Manufacturers	Germany
Hyundai Mipo Dockyard Co., Ltd.	Listed	Focus	9	Shipbuilding	Korea, Republic of
I.M.A. Industria Macchine Automatiche S.p.A.	Listed	Scale	7	Machinery	Italy
IAWS Group, plc	Listed	Scale	5	Wholesalers	Ireland
IBS	Listed	Focus	9	Electronics	Sweden
Idex Corporation	Listed	Scale	7	Machinery	United States
Idexx Laboratories Corp.	Listed	Scale	5	Instruments, Gauges & Meters	United States
IGM Financial Inc.	Listed	Scale	8	Financial Services	Canada
Imerys	Listed	Scale	6	Gypsum, Lumber & Building Supplies	France
Impac Mortgage Holdings, Inc.	Listed	Opening	3	Real Estate	United States
Independent News & Media PLC	Listed	Scale	6	Newspaper Publishers	Ireland
Indorama Group, The	Listed	Scale	6	Textiles	Indonesia
Inoplast	Non-listed	Scale	5	Chemicals	France
Insight	Listed	Scale	5	Wholesalers	United States
Integra Lifesciences Corporation	Listed	Scale	5	Medical, Surgical & Dental Suppliers	United States
Intraplas	Non-listed	Scale	5	Chemicals	Portugal
Intuit Inc.	Listed	Scale	8	Systems & Subsystems	United States
Irish Life & Permanent plc	Listed	Scale	5	Insurance Companies	Ireland
ISDIN	Non-listed	Scale	5	Pharma, Drugs & Health Care	Spain
IWKA AG	Listed	Scale	7	Machinery	Germany
J. & S. Sklavenitis S.A.	Non-listed	Scale	5	Department Stores	Greece
J. Jill Group Inc	Listed	Scale	6	Apparel Store Chains	United States
J.B. Hunt Transport Services, Inc.	Listed	Scale	5	Trucking	United States

Sources: Value Building Growth database; A.T. Kearney analysis

Appendix C. The 600 Stable Endgame Niche Fighters *(continued)*

Entity Name	Company Status	S-Curve (4 Phases)	S-Curve (16 Phases)	Industry	Country
J.M. Smucker Company, The	Listed	Scale	7	Canners & Processors	United States
J.W.Lees & CO.(Brewers) Limited	Non-listed	Scale	6	Brewers	United Kingdom
Jabil Circuit, Inc.	Listed	Scale	5	Original Parts & Accessories Mfrs.	United States
Japan Crown Cork Co.,Ltd.	Non-listed	Scale	5	Chemicals	Japan
Jefferies & Company, Inc.	Listed	Focus	9	Securities Brokerage	United States
Jeol Ltd.	Listed	Scale	5	Instruments, Gauges & Meters	Japan
John Q. Hammons Hotels	Listed	Scale	5	Hotel & Motel Chains	United States
Johnston Press plc.	Listed	Scale	6	Newspaper Publishers	United Kingdom
Jollibee Foods Corporation	Listed	Scale	5	Department Stores	Philippines
Kasai Kogyo Company Limited	Listed	Scale	5	Original Parts & Accessories Mfrs.	Japan
KB Home	Listed	Scale	5	Home Builders	United States
Keck Seng	Listed	Scale	6	Food	Malaysia
Kennametal Worldwide	Listed	Focus	9	Machine Tools	Germany
Kerry Group PLC	Listed	Scale	6	Food	Ireland
Kingboard Chemicals Holdings Ltd.	Listed	Scale	5	Metal Products	Hong Kong
Kingspan Group PLC	Listed	Opening	2	Construction	Ireland
Kinpo Electronics, Inc.	Listed	Focus	9	Electronic Data Processing Equipment	Taiwan, Province of China
Kinyosha Co.,Ltd.	Non-listed	Scale	5	Chemicals	Japan
Kioritz Corporation	Listed	Scale	7	Machinery	Japan
Kirii Construction Materials Co.,Ltd.	Non-listed	Scale	5	Metal Products	Japan
Kolt Transportation	Listed	Scale	5	Trucking	United States
Kolon Industries Company Limited	Listed	Scale	6	Textiles	Korea, Republic of
Kongsberg Gruppen	Listed	Scale	7	Machinery	Norway
Krones AG	Listed	Scale	7	Machinery	Germany
Kronos Incorporated	Listed	Focus	9	Electronics	United States
K-Swiss, Inc.	Listed	Focus	10	Shoe Manufacturers	United States
Kuehne & Nagel	Listed	Scale	8	Freight Forwarders	Switzerland
KV Pharmaceutical Company	Listed	Scale	5	Pharma, Drugs & Health Care	United States
KYB Co., Inc.	Listed	Scale	7	Machinery	Japan
Kyosan Electric Manufacturing Company Limited	Listed	Focus	9	Automatic Controls	Japan

Sources: Value Building Growth database; A.T. Kearney analysis

Appendix C. The 600 Stable Endgame Niche Fighters *(continued)*

Entity Name	Company Status	S-Curve (4 Phases)	S-Curve (16 Phases)	Industry	Country
Lan Airlines SA	Listed	Scale	5	Airlines	Chile
Landry's Restaurants, Inc.	Listed	Scale	5	Restaurants & Fast Food Franchisers	United States
Landstar Systems	Listed	Scale	5	Trucking	United States
Laureate Education, Inc.	Listed	Opening	3	Service Organisations	United States
Lee Enterprises	Listed	Scale	6	Newspaper Publishers	United States
Legg Mason	Listed	Focus	9	Securities Brokerage	United States
Lexar Media Inc.	Listed	Focus	11	Photographic Equipment & Supplies	United States
Lexmark International Group A	Listed	Focus	12	Business Machines & Office Equipment	United States
Liberty Medical	Listed	Scale	5	Pharma, Drugs & Health Care	United States
Linamar Corporation Inc.	Listed	Scale	7	Machinery	Canada
Lincare	Listed	Scale	6	Medical Services	United States
Lincoln Electric Company, The	Listed	Scale	6	Industrial & Comm Elect. Equipment	United States
Lindt & Sprungli	Listed	Scale	6	Confectionary Goods	Switzerland
Logista	Listed	Scale	5	Trucking	Spain
Logitech	Listed	Focus	9	Electronic Data Processing Equipment	Switzerland
Lopez Baena S.A.	Non-listed	Scale	5	Wholesalers	Spain
Lotte Chilsung Co., LTD.	Listed	Focus	9	Soft Drink Producers & Bottlers	Korea, Republic of
Love's Travel Stops & Country Store	Non-listed	Scale	5	Restaurants & Fast Food Franchisers	United States
LS Cable Ltd.	Listed	Focus	9	Power Transmission Equipment	Korea, Republic of
LS Industrial Systems Co., Ltd.	Listed	Scale	6	Industrial & Comm Elect. Equipment	Korea, Republic of
MAA Holdings Berhad	Listed	Scale	5	Insurance Companies	Malaysia
Maanshan Iron Steel Company Limited	Listed	Focus	9	Steel Producers	China
Macphie of Glenbervie Limited	Non-listed	Focus	11	Bakers	United Kingdom
Magellan Aerospace Corporation	Listed	Scale	6	Miscellaneous Aerospace	Canada
Mahle Metal Leve SA	Listed	Scale	5	Original Parts & Accessories Mfrs.	Brazil
Malakoff Berhad	Listed	Opening	2	Utilities	Malaysia
Man Group plc	Listed	Scale	8	Financial Services	United Kingdom
Manitowoc Company, Inc., The	Listed	Scale	7	Machinery	United States
Manufacturers and Traders Trust Company	Listed	Scale	5	Commercial Banks	United States
Marino de la Fuente SA	Non-listed	Scale	5	Wholesalers	Spain

Sources: Value Building Growth database; A.T. Kearney analysis

Appendix C. The 600 Stable Endgame Niche Fighters *(continued)*

Entity Name	Company Status	S-Curve (4 Phases)	S-Curve (16 Phases)	Industry	Country
Markel Corporation	Listed	Scale	5	Insurance Companies	United States
Mars Engineering Corporation	Listed	Scale	7	Machinery	Japan
Maruzen Petrochemical	Non-listed	Focus	9	Oil & Gas	Japan
Matrix Service Company	Listed	Opening	2	Construction	United States
Matsumoto Industry Co., Ltd.	Non-listed	Scale	5	Department Stores	Japan
Matthews International	Listed	Scale	5	Metal Products	United States
Mayr-Meinhof Karton AG	Listed	Scale	5	Packaging Products	Austria
McInherney Holdings PLC	Listed	Opening	2	Construction	Ireland
MDC Holdings Inc	Listed	Scale	5	Home Builders	United States
Medicis Pharmaceuticals Corporation	Listed	Scale	5	Pharma, Drugs & Health Care	United States
Mentor Corp.	Listed	Scale	5	Medical, Surgical & Dental Suppliers	United States
Mercury General Corporation	Listed	Scale	5	Insurance Companies	United States
Meritage Homes Corporation	Listed	Scale	5	Home Builders	United States
Metall ZUG Grupe	Listed	Focus	9	Appliances & Consumer Products	Switzerland
MGI Coutier	Listed	Scale	5	Original Parts & Accessories Mfrs.	France
Michaels Stores, Inc.	Listed	Scale	5	Department Stores	United States
Micros Systems, Inc.	Listed	Focus	12	Business Machines & Office Equipment	United States
Midland Cybernet Limited	Listed	Opening	3	Real Estate	Hong Kong
Miwa Lock Co.,Ltd.	Non-listed	Focus	9	Electronics	Japan
Mohawk Industries, Inc.	Listed	Scale	6	Furnishings	United States
Moog Inc.	Listed	Focus	12	Business Machines & Office Equipment	United States
Morgan Sindall PLC	Listed	Opening	2	Construction	United Kingdom
Mueller-Weingarten AG	Listed	Scale	7	Machinery	Germany
Mylan Inc.	Listed	Scale	5	Pharma, Drugs & Health Care	United States
National Foods Limited	Listed	Scale	6	Food	Australia
National Instruments Corp.	Listed	Focus	12	Business Machines & Office Equipment	United States
Navarre	Listed	Scale	5	Wholesalers	United States
NBTY Inc	Listed	Scale	5	Food	United States
Network Solutions	Listed	Scale	5	Pharma, Drugs & Health Care	United States
New York Community Bank	Listed	Focus	10	Savings & Loan	United States

Sources: Value Building Growth database; A.T. Kearney analysis

Appendix C. The 600 Stable Endgame Niche Fighters *(continued)*

Entity Name	Company Status	S-Curve (4 Phases)	S-Curve (16 Phases)	Industry	Country
Next Retail LTD.	Listed	Scale	5	Department Stores	United Kingdom
Nidec Copal Corp.	Listed	Focus	9	Electronics	Japan
Nihon Kohden Corporation	Listed	Scale	5	Instruments, Gauges & Meters	Japan
Nissin Food Products, Co., Ltd.	Listed	Scale	5	Commercial Banks	Japan
Nitori	Listed	Scale	5	Department Stores	Japan
Noble Foods Ltd	Non-listed	Scale	6	Food	United Kingdom
Nokian Tyres PLC	Listed	Focus	9	Rubber & Tire Mfrs.	Finland
North Fork Bank	Listed	Scale	5	Commercial Banks	United States
Northern Foods PLC	Listed	Scale	6	Food	United Kingdom
Ocean System Corporation	Non-listed	Scale	5	Department Stores	Japan
Odfjell	Listed	Scale	6	Shipping	Norway
Oil Search Limited	Listed	Focus	9	Oil & Gas	Australia
Okura Industrial Company Limited	Listed	Scale	7	Paint & Resin Manufacturers	Japan
Old Dominion Freight Line, Inc.	Listed	Scale	5	Trucking	United States
Olympus Corporation	Listed	Focus	11	Photographic Equipment & Supplies	Japan
OMC Card, Inc.	Listed	Scale	5	Commercial Banks	Japan
OptionCare, Inc.	Listed	Scale	6	Medical Services	United States
Orbital Sciences Corporation	Listed	Scale	6	Miscellaneous Aerospace	United States
O'Reilly Auto Parts	Listed	Scale	5	Department Stores	United States
Orion Corp.	Listed	Scale	6	Confectionary Goods	Korea, Republic of
Orion Group	Listed	Scale	5	Pharma, Drugs & Health Care	Finland
OSG Corporation	Listed	Focus	9	Machine Tools	Japan
Oshkosh Corporation	Listed	Focus	9	Truck & Trailer Manufacturers	United States
Overseas Shipholding Group, Inc.	Listed	Scale	6	Shipping	United States
P.A.M. Transportation Services, Inc.	Listed	Scale	5	Trucking	United States
Pacific Sunwear California Inc	Listed	Scale	6	Apparel Store Chains	United States
Paladin Resources plc	Listed	Focus	9	Oil & Gas	United Kingdom
Panariagroup Industrie Ceramiche S.P.A.	Non-listed	Scale	6	Gypsum, Lumber & Building Supplies	Italy
Patrick	Listed	Scale	8	Freight Forwarders	Australia
Patterson Companies, Inc.	Listed	Scale	5	Wholesalers	United States

Sources: Value Building Growth database; A.T. Kearney analysis

Appendix C. The 600 Stable Endgame Niche Fighters *(continued)*

Entity Name	Company Status	S-Curve (4 Phases)	S-Curve (16 Phases)	Industry	Country
PC Mall Sales, Inc.	Listed	Scale	5	Department Stores	United States
Peacock Group plc, The	Non-listed	Scale	6	Apparel Store Chains	United Kingdom
Pediatrix Medical Group	Listed	Scale	6	Medical Services	United States
PEI Licensing, Inc.	Listed	Scale	5	Wholesalers	United States
Pendragon PLC	Listed	Scale	5	Department Stores	United Kingdom
Penn National Gaming, Inc.	Listed	Scale	6	Recreation	United States
Penn Virginia Corporation	Listed	Focus	9	Oil & Gas	United States
Penn West Energy Trust	Listed	Focus	9	Oil & Gas	Canada
Perdigao SA	Listed	Focus	9	Meat Packers	Brazil
Petroleum Development Corporation	Listed	Focus	9	Exploration, Drilling Service & Equipment	United States
Petsmart Store Support Group, Inc.	Listed	Scale	5	Department Stores	United States
Philadelphia Insurance Companies	Listed	Scale	5	Insurance Companies	United States
Phoenix Healthcare Distribution Limited	Non-listed	Scale	5	Wholesalers	United Kingdom
Pilkington Group Limited	Non-listed	Focus	9	Glass	United Kingdom
Pirkanmaan Osuuskauppa	Non-listed	Scale	5	Department Stores	Finland
Pool Corporation	Listed	Scale	5	Wholesalers	United States
Porsche AG	Listed	Scale	7	Automotive Manufacturers	Germany
PPB Group Berhad	Listed	Scale	6	Food	Malaysia
PPG Industries	Non-listed	Scale	5	Chemicals	Spain
Praxair Technology, Inc.	Non-listed	Scale	5	Chemicals	Spain
Pretoria Port Cement Company Limited	Listed	Scale	6	Cement Producers	South Africa
Pride International, Inc.	Listed	Focus	9	Exploration, Drilling Service & Equipment	United States
ProAssurance Corp.	Listed	Scale	5	Insurance Companies	United States
Progressive Casualty Insurance Company	Listed	Scale	5	Insurance Companies	United States
PTT Exploration And Production Public Co	Listed	Focus	9	Oil & Gas	Thailand
Publix Asset Management Company	Non-listed	Scale	5	Wholesalers	United States
Puma AG	Listed	Focus	10	Shoe Manufacturers	Germany
Punch Taverns (PTL) Limited	Non-listed	Scale	6	Food	United Kingdom
PZ Cussons	Listed	Scale	5	Cosmetics & Toiletries	United Kingdom
Quiksilver, Inc.	Listed	Scale	5	Apparel Manufacturers	United States

Sources: Value Building Growth database; A.T. Kearney analysis

221

Appendix C. The 600 Stable Endgame Niche Fighters *(continued)*

Entity Name	Company Status	S-Curve (4 Phases)	S-Curve (16 Phases)	Industry	Country
QuikTrip Corporation	Non-listed	Focus	9	Oil & Gas	United States
Radian Group Inc.	Listed	Scale	5	Insurance Companies	United States
Rainbow Chicken Limited	Listed	Focus	9	Meat Packers	South Africa
Ramside Hall Hotel	Non-listed	Scale	5	Hotel & Motel Chains	United Kingdom
Ranbaxy Laboratories Limited	Listed	Scale	5	Pharma, Drugs & Health Care	India
Readymix Asland SA	Non-listed	Scale	6	Gypsum, Lumber & Building Supplies	Spain
Recordati S.p.A.	Listed	Scale	5	Medical, Surgical & Dental Suppliers	Italy
Reinsurance Group Of America Incorporated	Listed	Scale	5	Insurance Companies	United States
Reitman's Limited	Listed	Scale	6	Apparel Store Chains	Canada
Renishaw PLC	Listed	Scale	5	Instruments, Gauges & Meters	United Kingdom
Respironics	Listed	Scale	5	Medical, Surgical & Dental Suppliers	United States
Restaurant Group PLC	Listed	Scale	5	Restaurants & Fast Food Franchisers	United Kingdom
Reyal Urbis	Listed	Opening	3	Real Estate	Spain
Richter Gedeon	Listed	Scale	5	Pharma, Drugs & Health Care	Hungary
Rieber & SON ASA	Listed	Scale	6	Food	Norway
RLI Corp.	Listed	Scale	5	Insurance Companies	United States
Robert Wiseman Dairies PLC	Listed	Scale	6	Dairy Products	United Kingdom
ROK	Listed	Opening	2	Construction	United Kingdom
Roper Industries Income	Listed	Scale	7	Machinery	United States
Rosehill Polymers Ltd	Non-listed	Scale	5	Chemicals	United Kingdom
Rotork	Listed	Focus	9	Electronics	United Kingdom
Royal Unibrew A/S	Listed	Scale	6	Brewers	Denmark
Rubiera Burgos SA	Non-listed	Scale	6	Gypsum, Lumber & Building Supplies	Spain
Russel Metals	Listed	Scale	5	Wholesalers	Canada
SafeNet Inc.	Listed	Focus	9	Electronics	United States
Saint Jude Medical, Inc.	Listed	Scale	5	Medical, Surgical & Dental Suppliers	United States
Saint Lawrence Cement Group Inc	Listed	Scale	6	Cement Producers	Canada
Saint-Gobain Oberland	Listed	Focus	9	Glass	Germany
Salton Holdings Limited	Non-listed	Focus	9	Electronics	United Kingdom
Samworth Brothers	Non-listed	Scale	6	Food	United Kingdom

Sources: Value Building Growth database; A.T. Kearney analysis

Appendix C. The 600 Stable Endgame Niche Fighters *(continued)*

Entity Name	Company Status	S-Curve (4 Phases)	S-Curve (16 Phases)	Industry	Country
Sanderson Farms, Incorporated	Listed	Scale	7	Canners & Processors	United States
SanDisk Corporation	Listed	Scale	5	Original Parts & Accessories Mfrs.	United States
Sanfilippo John B & Son, Inc.	Listed	Scale	7	Canners & Processors	United States
Sanyo Shinpan Finance Company Ltd	Listed	Scale	5	Commercial Banks	Japan
Sasol Limited	Listed	Scale	5	Chemicals	South Africa
Scansource Inc.	Listed	Scale	5	Wholesalers	United States
Schein Henry Inc	Listed	Scale	5	Wholesalers	United States
Schibsted ASA	Listed	Scale	6	Newspaper Publishers	Norway
Schuitema NV	Listed	Scale	5	Wholesalers	Netherlands
Scribona AB	Listed	Scale	5	Wholesalers	Sweden
Seaboard Corporation	Listed	Scale	6	Food	United States
Seco Tools AB	Listed	Focus	9	Machine Tools	Sweden
Siemens Healthcare Diagnostics, Inc.	Listed	Scale	5	Medical, Surgical & Dental Suppliers	United States
Select Medical Corporation	Non-listed	Scale	6	Medical Services	United States
Sembcorp Marine Limited	Listed	Focus	9	Shipbuilding	Singapore
Semperit AG Holding	Listed	Focus	9	Rubber & Tire Mfrs.	Austria
Senju Metal Industry Co.,Ltd.	Non-listed	Scale	5	Metal Products	Japan
Sepracor Inc.	Listed	Scale	5	Pharma, Drugs & Health Care	United States
Severfield-Rowen PLC	Listed	Opening	2	Construction	United Kingdom
Shenzhen Nanshan Power Electric 'A	Listed	Opening	2	Utilities	China
Shin Kurushima Dockyard Co.,Ltd.	Non-listed	Focus	9	Shipbuilding	Japan
Shinsegae	Listed	Scale	5	Department Stores	Korea, Republic of
SIA Engineering Company	Listed	Scale	6	Miscellaneous Aerospace	Singapore
Siam City Cement	Listed	Scale	6	Cement Producers	Thailand
SIG	Listed	Scale	7	Machinery	Switzerland
SIG plc	Listed	Opening	2	Construction	United Kingdom
Simpson Manufacturing Co., Inc.	Listed	Opening	2	Construction	United States
Singulus Technologies Aktiengesellschaft	Listed	Scale	7	Machinery	Germany
Sinopec Shanghai Petrochemicals	Listed	Scale	5	Chemicals	China
Sligro Food Group N.V.	Listed	Scale	5	Wholesalers	Netherlands

Sources: Value Building Growth database; A.T. Kearney analysis

Appendix C. The 600 Stable Endgame Niche Fighters *(continued)*

Entity Name	Company Status	S-Curve (4 Phases)	S-Curve (16 Phases)	Industry	Country
SNL Financial LC	Listed	Scale	5	Commercial Banks	United States
Sociedad Espanola de Carburos Metalicos SA	Non-listed	Scale	5	Chemicals	Spain
Sociedad Iberica de Construcciones Electricas SA	Non-listed	Focus	9	Electronics	Spain
Societe BIC	Listed	Scale	5	Wholesalers	France
Sodexho	Non-listed	Scale	5	Hotel & Motel Chains	Italy
Sogefi Spa	Listed	Scale	5	Original Parts & Accessories Mfrs.	Italy
Sonic Healthcare Limited	Listed	Scale	6	Medical Services	Australia
South Financial Group Inc	Listed	Scale	5	Commercial Banks	United States
Spir Communication	Listed	Scale	6	Newspaper Publishers	France
Spirax-Sarco Engineering PLC	Listed	Focus	9	Machine Tools	United Kingdom
Stanley Electric Company Limited	Listed	Scale	5	Original Parts & Accessories Mfrs.	Japan
Starbucks Corp.	Listed	Scale	5	Department Stores	United States
Station Casinos	Listed	Scale	5	Hotel & Motel Chains	United States
Steak 'N Shake Company	Listed	Scale	5	Restaurants & Fast Food Franchisers	United States
Steris Corporation	Listed	Scale	5	Medical, Surgical & Dental Suppliers	United States
Steve Madden	Listed	Focus	9	Shoe Retailers	United States
Stryker	Listed	Scale	5	Medical, Surgical & Dental Suppliers	United States
Sudamericana De Vapores	Listed	Scale	6	Shipping	Chile
Suncor Energy Inc.	Listed	Focus	9	Oil & Gas	Canada
SVO Energie GmbH	Non-listed	Focus	9	Oil & Gas	Germany
Sygnity	Listed	Focus	9	Electronic Data Processing Equipment	Poland
Symantec Corp.	Listed	Scale	8	Systems & Subsystems	United States
Sysco Corp.	Listed	Scale	5	Wholesalers	United States
T.Clarke	Listed	Scale	6	Electrical	United Kingdom
Tabcorp Holdings Limited	Listed	Scale	6	Recreation	Australia
Tachi-S Company Limited	Listed	Scale	5	Original Parts & Accessories Mfrs.	Japan
Taekwang Industrial Co.	Listed	Scale	6	Textiles	Korea, Republic of
Taito Corp.	Listed	Scale	7	Games & Toys	Japan
Takara Company Limited	Listed	Scale	7	Games & Toys	Japan
Tamron Co., Ltd.	Listed	Focus	11	Photographic Equipment & Supplies	Japan

Sources: Value Building Growth database; A.T. Kearney analysis

Appendix C. The 600 Stable Endgame Niche Fighters *(continued)*

Entity Name	Company Status	S-Curve (4 Phases)	S-Curve (16 Phases)	Industry	Country
Tan Chong Motor Centre	Listed	Scale	7	Automotive Manufacturers	Malaysia
Tandberg	Listed	Focus	9	Electronics	Taiwan, Province of China
Taylor & Francis Group	Non-listed	Scale	6	Newspaper Publishers	United Kingdom
Teva Pharmaceutical Industries Ltd.	Listed	Scale	6	Gypsum, Lumber & Building Supplies	Hong Kong
Texas Regional Bankshares Inc	Listed	Scale	5	Commercial Banks	United States
Textil Santanderina	Non-listed	Scale	5	Apparel Fabrics	Spain
Thai Union Frozen Products	Listed	Scale	7	Canners & Processors	Thailand
TheTempoGroup.net	Listed	Scale	5	Pharma, Drugs & Health Care	Indonesia
Thor Industries, Inc.	Listed	Focus	9	Truck & Trailer Manufacturers	United States
Tietoenator	Listed	Focus	12	Business Machines & Office Equipment	Finland
TJX Companies, Inc.	Listed	Scale	5	Department Stores	United States
Todymas SA	Non-listed	Scale	5	Department Stores	Spain
Tokai Kogyo Co.,Ltd.	Non-listed	Scale	5	Chemicals	Japan
Toll Holdings Limited	Listed	Scale	8	Freight Forwarders	Australia
Topcon Corporation	Listed	Focus	9	Electronics	Japan
Torm	Listed	Scale	6	Shipping	Denmark
Torstar Corp.	Listed	Scale	6	Newspaper Publishers	Canada
Toyo Denka Kogyo Co., Ltd.	Non-listed	Scale	5	Metal Products	Japan
Transat AT Inc	Listed	Scale	5	Airlines	Canada
Trinity Mirror PLC	Listed	Scale	6	Newspaper Publishers	United Kingdom
Tsingtao Brewery Company Limited	Listed	Scale	6	Brewers	China
Tsurumi Sunmarine Co., Ltd.	Non-listed	Scale	5	Trucking	Japan
Tuesday Morning	Listed	Focus	11	Discount Stores	United States
U-MING MARINE TRANSPORT CORP.	Listed	Scale	6	Shipping	Taiwan, Province of China
UMW	Listed	Scale	7	Automotive Manufacturers	Malaysia
Uni-Select Inc.	Listed	Scale	5	Wholesalers	Canada
United Drug	Listed	Scale	5	Medical, Surgical & Dental Suppliers	Ireland
Urenco Limited	Non-listed	Scale	5	Chemicals	United Kingdom
US Xpress Enterprises Inc	Listed	Scale	5	Trucking	United States
U-Shin Limited	Listed	Scale	5	Wholesalers	Japan

Sources: Value Building Growth database; A.T. Kearney analysis

225

Appendix C. The 600 Stable Endgame Niche Fighters *(continued)*

Entity Name	Company Status	S-Curve (4 Phases)	S-Curve (16 Phases)	Industry	Country
Valero Energy Corp.	Listed	Focus	9	Oil & Gas	United States
Valspar Corp.	Listed	Scale	7	Paint & Resin Manufacturers	United States
Veidekke ASA	Listed	Opening	2	Construction	Norway
Velamen SA	Non-listed	Scale	6	Textiles	Spain
Vestas Wind Systems A/S	Non-listed	Scale	6	Electrical	Denmark
Vilmorin	Listed	Scale	5	Wholesalers	France
Vina Concha Y Toro	Listed	Focus	10	Distillers	Chile
Vivartia	Non-listed	Scale	6	Food	Greece
Votorantim Celulose	Listed	Scale	6	Printing & Writing Paper	Brazil
W Holding Company, Inc.	Listed	Scale	5	Commercial Banks	United States
W.R. Berkley Corporation	Listed	Scale	5	Insurance Companies	United States
Walsin Lihwa Corp.	Listed	Focus	9	Wire, Chain & Spring	Taiwan, Province of China
Wawa	Non-listed	Scale	5	Restaurants & Fast Food Franchisers	United States
WEG	Listed	Scale	6	Industrial & Comm Elect. Equipment	Brazil
Weir Group PLC	Listed	Scale	7	Machinery	United Kingdom
Werner Enterprises Inc	Listed	Scale	5	Trucking	United States
Western Refining	Listed	Focus	9	Oil & Gas	United States
Whitbread Hotel Company Limited	Non-listed	Scale	5	Hotel & Motel Chains	United Kingdom
Whole Foods Market Inc	Listed	Scale	5	Department Stores	United States
William Demant Holding A/S	Listed	Scale	5	Instruments, Gauges & Meters	Denmark
William Kenyon & Sons Limited	Non-listed	Scale	6	Textiles	United States
Williams Sonoma Inc	Listed	Scale	5	Department Stores	United States
Wolseley PLC	Listed	Scale	5	Wholesalers	United Kingdom
Wolverine Worldwide Inc	Listed	Focus	10	Shoe Manufacturers	United States
Yakult Honsha Company Limited	Listed	Scale	6	Dairy Products	Japan
Yamashita Rubber Co.,Ltd.	Non-listed	Scale	5	Chemicals	Japan
Yang Ming Marine Transport Corp.	Listed	Scale	6	Shipping	Taiwan, Province of China
Zara Espana SA	Non-listed	Scale	6	Apparel Store Chains	Spain
Zebra Technologies Corp.	Listed	Scale	6	Electrical	United States
Zeus Quimica SA	Non-listed	Scale	5	Wholesalers	Spain

Sources: Value Building Growth database; A.T. Kearney analysis

|Index

Page numbers in **bold** indicate tables and figures; n indicates a footnote.

|About the Authors

Dr. Fritz Kroeger is vice president of A.T. Kearney in Germany. He is a senior management consultant and specialist in growth and strategic development and has worked in Europe, the United States, and Japan since 1976. He is author or coauthor of eight books on restructuring, growth strategy, and merger integration, including *Winning the Merger Endgame: A Playbook for Profiting from Industry Consolidation* (McGraw-Hill, 2002) and *Stretch! How Great Companies Grow in Good Times and Bad* (John Wiley & Sons, 2004). In 2004, Fritz was chosen by *Consulting Magazine* for its annual list of the Top 25 Most Influential Consultants.

Michael Moriarty is a vice president of A.T. Kearney in the United States, and leads A.T. Kearney's consumer industries and retail practice. He specializes in dramatic business performance improvement and innovative partnering strategies. Mike has more than 30 years of industry and consulting experience in the fast-moving consumer products and retail industries, and has served clients in Europe, Asia, and the Americas. He is a frequent speaker and is the author of *Power Play: The Beginning of the Endgame in Net Markets* (John Wiley & Sons, 2001).

Dr. Andrej Vizjak is a vice president in A.T. Kearney's Munich office, and leads the firm's Eastern European unit with 10 years of consulting experience. He regularly publishes articles on strategic management and growth, and is the author of two books on growth strategies, the most recent of which is *Media Management: Leveraging Content for Profitable Growth* (Springer, 2003).